Prepare for Persecution

(Revised and Expanded Edition)

Maria Kneas

Forward by Douglas J. Hagmann

Prepare for Persecution
(Revised and Expanded Edition)

Copyright © 2016 by Maria M. Kneas and Douglas J. Hagmann.

Maria Kneas is also the author of
How to Fight Discouragement.

All Scripture quotations are from the King James Version of the *Holy Bible*.

ISBN-13: 978-1539446583
ISBN-10: 1539446581

*Dedicated to faithful watchmen,
to pastors who have the courage to preach Biblically,
and to all Bible-believing Christians who want to be
faithful to God and to one another.*

*Also dedicated to my husband Ray, who is in Heaven.
Ray fought the good fight, he kept the faith, and he
endured to the end. (2 Timothy 4:7; Matthew 24:13)
May we do the same.*

*"Never be afraid to trust
an unknown future
to a known God."*

(Corrie ten Boom)

Contents

Foreword by Douglas J. Hagmann 7
Preface 10

We Are Living In Perilous Times

1. Understanding the Times 15
2. Brainwashing Christians..25
3. Thought Police In Colleges 29
4. Teaching Kids To Be Sociopaths 33
5. A Biblical Warning For America 38
6. Heading Towards Dictatorship................................52
7. Mainstreaming Occultism 66
8. Bathroom Battles and College Chaos.....................77

Biblical Encouragement & Guidance

9. Dealing With Shock 87
10. Fighting Fear 94
11. Handling Grief...111
12. The Bottom Line...116
13. Renewing Our Minds 122
14. Building Faith..134
15. Learning To Trust God More 142
16. Do We Love God?...156
17. Don't Give The Devil A Beachhead......................166
18. Giving Thanks To God 183

19. Jesus Told Us To Forgive 192
20. The Importance of Integrity 200
21. Loving Difficult People.. 204
22. The Antidote to Humanism................................... 210
23. A Biblical Approach to Pain 216
24. The Big Picture — Eternity................................... 228
25. The Challenge 233
26. Helping Others Stand Firm 235

Appendix A. Goddess Worship In America................. 237
Appendix B. Darwin's Deadly Legacy 246
Appendix C. Resources 249

Notes... 251

*"Yea, though I walk through the
valley of the shadow of death,
I will fear no evil:
for thou art with me;
thy rod and thy staff they comfort me."*
(Psalm 23:4)

Foreword by
Douglas J. Hagmann

Prepare for Persecution is an extremely important informational, instructional and inspirational resource for all Christians living today. Unlike many books that tend to lose their relevance over time, its importance will increase exponentially in the coming days. It not only serves as a historical bookmark that illustrates the incremental progression of oppression against Christians, but provides sound biblical advice and encouragement as the persecution of Christians becomes more aggressive.

"Something wicked this way comes." That simple line, most commonly attributed to Shakespeare's *Macbeth*, seems to concisely summarize the ominous undertones of today's headlines and news stories. It also captures the feelings of many people who sense that something big is about to happen that will forever change life as we know it.

Most of us who are paying attention to current events, reading the headlines and listening to the uncensored news are waiting for this big, life altering event. Although such an event will undoubtedly happen, we tend to lose sight of the smaller, less dramatic yet equally destructive events that escape our attention in the interim. That is exactly how we have arrived at this moment in time.

While waiting for the dramatic and unmistakable "flash-bang" that will accompany and announce such an event, we have failed to see the evil subtleties that have been incrementally implemented against Bible-believing Christians everywhere, especially in the United States. We think that "it cannot happen here" when considering the persecution of Christians, or people being marginalized and vilified for adhering to the fundamental teachings in the Holy Bible. As this book clearly outlines, it not only ***can*** happen here, but it ***is*** happening here. Many Christians, however, are willfully choosing not to acknowledge our current path of immorality and lawlessness, which has created fertile ground for the evil to take root, grow and multiply.

As a detective working in the field for the last three decades, I've seen a lot of cases brought before various courts. Their outcomes were decided on the weight of the evidence submitted before judges and juries. Based on my experience in these venues, I can state with authority that the contents of this book would effectively convince any judge or jury that Bible-believing Christians are being persecuted for their beliefs in the United States and all throughout the Western world. It has convinced me, and it will undoubtedly convince you, the reader as well.

Even more troubling is that the level of persecution against Christians remains unfettered and is being ramped-up on a near daily basis. The author presents a strong case for not just this continuing course of egregiousness, but for the future course of blatant persecution that will undoubtedly confront all of us. Bible-believing and practicing Christians are being forced to acquiesce to principles antithetical to our faith and most importantly, deadly to our eternal salvation. It is an insidious tactic that is being done under the guise of tolerance, social justice, and other "buzz words" and phrases that are commonly used to hide the true intent of an agenda so evil, and a lie so big, that few believe it exists.

Having gone from an investigator to the host of a weekday radio talk show, I am often confronted with a recurring question from countless listeners who ask, "How can I wake up my family, friends or neighbors to the events that are taking place?" I am now able to provide them with the answer by recommending this book with complete confidence and without reservation.

Prepare for Persecution serves as the perfect "wake-up call" for all Christians, from the most well-informed to those who are just now waking up to what's going on around them. Like a flawless courtroom exhibit upon which a litigant rests their case, it covers the most critical aspects of the war against Christians

Foreword

with just the right amount of detail and documentation. It makes an airtight case that will remain relevant throughout our history.

There's more, however, than just merely waking up or alerting others to the level of persecution we are currently experiencing, and which will grow exponentially worse as prophesied in the Holy Bible. While it's necessary to understand how we arrived here and identify the plots, plans and schemes of those whose agenda it is to silence and persecute Christians, it's of critical importance to know how we must prepare ourselves spiritually and emotionally for what is yet to come.

In fact, the second most common question I receive as a radio talk show host broadcasting across an array of Christian networks is, "What can I do to prepare, or how can I fight or make a difference?" Again, I am now able to provide an answer by recommending this book. *Prepare for Persecution* serves as a critically important field manual and guide to becoming spiritually and emotionally prepared.

Rarely do we find a resource that combines vital, foundational information about such a crucial issue with sound biblical instruction and inspiration. *Prepare for Persecution* is exactly that resource. It will provide you with information, instruction and inspiration to help you confront what lies ahead.

Douglas J. Hagmann
Host, The Hagmann & Hagmann Report

Preface

Many Christians sense that we are coming under persecution, but they only see bits and pieces of the problems. They have an uneasiness, but don't really know why.

Prepare for Persecution gives an overview of the problems. We are in the early stages of persecution, and it is increasing. Therefore, Christians need to be prepared to stand their ground in the face of pressure to go against their beliefs and moral convictions.

Christians in nations where there is persecution often say, "We never thought it could happen here." And they also say, "Why didn't anybody prepare us?"

Preparing for persecution, or any other kind of trial, depends on having a right relationship with God. We need to be born-again Christians who read the Bible, study it, and pray about it. God can lead us to the Scripture passages that we need, and His Holy Spirit can give us understanding of how to apply them to our lives.

Books, sermons, and other teachings by fellow Christians can be helpful. However, nothing and nobody can begin to compare with the Word of God and the leading of the Holy Spirit.

It is my hope and prayer that this book will help prepare you spiritually and emotionally for dealing with persecution. When the world tries to pressure us to deny our Christian faith, or to do things that go against Biblical standards of morality, then we need to stand our ground and refuse to compromise. We need to have spiritual backbone. We need to stand firm in our faith.

Psalm 2 is a good description of what is going on in the world today. Its relevance will be even more clear if you see the word "king" as including presidents, prime ministers, "banksters," power elites, etc. It says:

"Why do the heathen rage, and the people imagine a vain thing? The kings of the earth set themselves, and the rulers take counsel together, against the LORD, and against his anointed" (Psalm 2:1-2)

Throughout history, some people have conspired to overthrow God's people. Unless they repent and turn to God, these rebels will come to a bad end:

"Thou shalt break them with a rod of iron: thou shalt dash them in pieces like a potter's vessel." (Psalm 2:9)

In contrast, those who are faithful to God will rejoice for all Eternity:

"But as it is written, Eye hath not seen, nor ear heard, neither have entered into the heart of man, the things which God hath prepared for them that love him." (1 Corinthians 2:9)

*"If God be for us,
who can be against us?"*
(Romans 8:31)

We Are Living In Perilous Times

*"These things I have spoken unto you,
that in me ye might have peace.
In the world ye shall have tribulation:
but be of good cheer;
I have overcome the world."*
(John 16:33)

Chapter 1

Understanding The Times

I was the first Christian in my family. Around 1982, my Mom and Dad (who were in their mid-sixties) began reading the Bible. They became so excited that they eagerly devoured it. My Dad would come running into the room saying, "Look at this!" and share a Scripture passage that really hit him.

As Mom and Dad shared their new-found enthusiasm for the Bible, their love bloomed. They enjoyed Prairie Home Companion, and when old timey music came on the radio, Dad would grab Mom and dance with her. He was always bringing her flowers from their garden.

They found a good church where the preaching was Biblical. Dad's enthusiasm for Scripture kept growing, and he got a master's degree in Biblical Studies. For the rest of their lives (into their nineties), Mom and Dad read a lot of Scripture every day, and often talked about it during meal time.

Sadly, times have changed. If Mom and Dad had discovered the Bible in 2014, they would probably have had difficulty finding a church with Biblical preaching. And the last time I listened to Prairie Home Companion, the humor had become raunchy.

People on TV now boast about doing things that you could have blackmailed them for 30 years ago. Many previously "unthinkable" things are becoming commonplace.

This didn't just happen by chance. I'm going to give you some disturbing information, accompanied by this Biblical reminder. Jesus told us to love our enemies and to pray for them. (Matthew 5:44) We should also do reasonable things to protect ourselves and to try to thwart their anti-Christian agenda, because Jesus told us to flee persecution when we can. (Matthew 10:23)

But that only applies if we can do it without denying our Lord. (Matthew 10:32-33)

Humanism is the mortal enemy of Christianity. It denies the existence of God and opposes Biblical morality.

Humanism says that man is basically good, but the Bible says that we are all sinners who need a Savior. We need to have God change our hearts. We need to become children of God.

Dr. Brock Chisholm is a psychiatrist. He was the first Secretary-General of the United Nations' World Health Organization. He demonstrated humanism's antipathy to the idea that men need a Savior when he said:

> "For many generations we have bowed our necks to the yoke of the conviction of sin. We have swallowed all manner of poisonous certainties fed us by our parents..."[1]

> "If the race is to be freed from its crippling burden of good and evil, it must be psychiatrists who take the original responsibility."[2]

Evidently, for Dr. Chisholm, "mental health" means not being able to become convicted of sin, and it also means not recognizing the difference between good and evil. According to American law, the inability to tell the difference between good and evil is the definition of "criminal insanity."

Dr. Chisholm made these statements in 1946. Therefore, the United Nations has had many years to try to change every country in ways that make it more difficult for its citizens to recognize the difference between good and evil. That could explain a lot of the crazy things that we see going on in the world today.

In America, humanism has been declared by the courts to be a tax-exempt religion.[3] This religion is openly hostile to Christianity. Its antagonism can be seen in the following quotations from humanists:

"The classroom must and will become the arena of conflict between the old and the new—the rotting corpse of Christianity... and the new faith of humanism."[4]

"Some opponents of Humanism have accused us of wishing to overthrow the traditional Christian family. They are right. That is exactly what we intend to do."[5]

In 1933, *The Humanist Manifesto* was written, stating the beliefs and goals of humanism.[6] One of the signers was John Dewey, who is called the "father of progressive education." He revolutionized education in America. Dewey was determined to use the school system to promote humanism.[7] Unfortunately, he succeeded.

For generations, American children have been taught humanist beliefs and values in public schools. Their Christian morals have been undermined by "values clarification" and other techniques.[8] Thomas Sowell said:

"The techniques of brainwashing developed in totalitarian countries are routinely used in psychological conditioning programs imposed on American school children."[9]

This results in radically changing the beliefs and moral values of the children. The brainwashing techniques used on our children result in the "acceptance of alternative values by psychological rather than rational means."[10]

In addition, there are people who call themselves atheists, but they hate God. (How can they hate somebody who doesn't exist? At some level, they must know that God is real.)

Look at the following quotation from 1977. The militant atheists have been working on this agenda for a long time now:

"We must ask how we can kill the God of Christianity. We need only to insure that our schools teach only secular knowledge."[11]

With such overt hostility to Christianity from humanists and atheists, who use the public schools to promote their agenda, it is not surprising that America has gone downhill spiritually and morally. For example, when I was in high school (1958-1961), there were only a few girls who were not virgins, and everybody knew who they were. They had "a reputation." Fast-forward 40 years to the year 2000 when my nephew got married. He and his wife were both virgins, and that was so unusual that people made a big deal out of it.

To see the extent of the change that has taken place in the United States, look at Yale University. It was founded by ministers in 1701 in order to spread Christianity. All students were required to "live religious, Godly and blameless lives according to the rules of God's word." They were told to spend time in prayer and reading Scripture, both publicly and in private. The stated goal of their studies was "to know God in Jesus Christ" and "to lead a Godly, sober life."[12]

And what is Yale like today, in modern America? In March 2013, students at Yale University attended a four-day workshop called "Sex Weekend." This event was led by a "sexologist," who gave the students "sensitivity training" in "sexual diversity." The students were taught to accept homosexuality, sadomasochism, bestiality (sex with animals), incest, and prostitution. Over half of Yale's students said that they had engaged in "consensual pain" (sadomasochism), and three percent said that they had sex with an animal.[13]

With humanists using the schools to try to undermine Christianity, it is not surprising that many people who were raised in Christian families do not share the faith of their parents and grandparents. According to a 2006 study by the Barna Group, the majority of today's young adults were involved in church and other Christian activities as teenagers. However, when they grew older, most of them became "spiritually disengaged." Among young adults who had a Christian background, only one out of five "maintained a level of spiritual activity consistent with their high school experiences."

The Barna study also showed that three out of four American teenagers have engaged in "psychic or witchcraft-related activity." (This does not include reading horoscopes and exposure to occult media.) One out of ten participated in a seance, and one out of twelve tried to cast a spell or mix a magic potion. More than a third used a Ouija board, and more than a third read a book about Wicca (a religion that is based on witchcraft and goddess worship).[14] Occultism is becoming mainstream.

That study was done in 2006, which was nine years ago. If the same study was done today, I would expect to see the results be even worse, because occultism is being openly promoted by the entertainment industry. It is also being taught in universities and nursing schools. You can read about that in *Goddess Unmasked* by Dr. Philip G. Davis (Spence Publishing Company, 1999).

Things have now gotten to the point that there is a movement to normalize pedophilia. Instead of wanting to protect children from sexual predators, some psychologists and academics want to protect the sexual rights of pedophiles, which they have rebranded as being "minor-attracted persons" who have a sexual orientation that should be respected.[15]

As a result of America's moral and spiritual free fall, we now see blatant hostility towards Christianity. For example, in 2001, a man in my church was sent to prison. Some of us visited him and asked if we could give him a magazine. The prison officials told us that we could do that, as long as it came directly from the publisher and the magazine was "appropriate." I asked them what "appropriate" meant and was told that pornography and violent material were not allowed.

We subscribed to a Christian magazine, to be sent to him directly by the publisher. The prison refused that magazine and sent it back. Evidently, somebody at that prison considered Christian writings to be "inappropriate." They treated it the same way that they treat pornography, by refusing to let him have it.

I talked about this with a friend from church whose son was in prison. She told me that her son was not allowed to have a Bible. His prison was full of Muslim literature and Wiccan writings, but Bibles were not allowed.

Some persecution takes the form of pressuring Christians to do things that are contrary to their religious convictions. For example, a Catholic nurse was forced to assist in performing an abortion. If she refused, she would be fired. She complied, but regrets it, and is now suing the hospital. This is part of a larger problem. The ACLU is trying to force Catholic hospitals to perform abortions.[16]

Sixty-three Christian businesses have lawsuits about provisions in ObamaCare that would force them to go against their religious convictions. One attorney said:

> "The United States government is taking the remarkable position that private individuals lose their religious freedom when they make a living."[17]

Jack Phillips is a Christian baker who works in Denver, Colorado. He politely refused to bake a wedding cake for a homosexual couple, saying that he would be happy to bake things for them "for any other occasion." There were demonstrations outside his shop, and he received so many death threats that he called the police. Then the couple charged him with discrimination. The judge ruled that if he refuses to make wedding cakes for homosexual marriages, then he will be fined and he might be sent to prison. The baker said that he would rather go to jail than violate his religious beliefs.[18]

Elaine and Jonathan Huguenin are Christians, and the owners of Elane Photography. In 2006, they turned down a request to do wedding photos for a same-sex marriage. This case went all the way to the New Mexico Supreme Court, which ruled against them. One of the judges said that the Huegenins are **"compelled by law to compromise the very religious beliefs that inspire their lives."** Their attorney said:

> "If Elane Photographer does not have her rights of conscience protected, then basically nobody does."

> "Americans are now on notice that the price of doing business is their freedom."[19]

If such things can be done to bakers and photographers, then what will happen to pastors and priests and rabbis who refuse to marry homosexual couples? What will happen to freedom of religion?

Using the courts to try to force people to endorse homosexuality is done by militant homosexual activists, as opposed to homosexuals who just want to be left alone to live their own lifestyle. The radical activists want to force everybody else to actively support what they are doing.

In contrast, that baker had turned down requests for wedding cakes from a number of other homosexual couples who respected his right to see things differently than they do. They just quietly looked for another baker who would be happy to get their business.

When I was a freshman in college (1961-1962), I had a friend there named Jessica. She was bisexual. Back then, I had never heard that term before. I didn't even know that such a thing existed before I became friends with her.

She was desperately looking for love, and had become promiscuous. Men would use her and treat her like trash. When that became too painful, then Jessica would turn to women. But then she would get hurt by them, and go back to men again. It was a cycle of pain, going back and forth between men and women, and getting hurt by them all.

Jessica was a sweet, vulnerable girl, and her heart was broken by so many people. I wish I could have helped her back then, but I didn't know how. If Jessica married a lesbian, she would never try to force a baker to make a wedding cake for her. She cared about other people, and respected them.

I've often thought about Jessica over the years, and prayed for her. I hope that she found the Lord.

During the recent government shutdown, the military chaplains were banned from performing any kind of services or ministry on military bases. They were not even allowed to minister as volunteers (which would not cost the Pentagon a penny), and they were threatened with arrest if they did any ministry on base. Congressman Tim Huelskamp said:

"Time and time again this Administration demonstrates it is waging a war against the very religious freedoms upon which America was founded." [20]

Obviously this had nothing to do with saving money, because the chaplains offered to serve for free as volunteers. In addition, it costs money to arrest people and hold them in jail, and it is expensive to have lawyers prosecute them. So this was overt persecution of Christians. And it was done by our government, to the men and women who risk life and limb in order to protect our nation. They also risk getting post traumatic stress disorder, which is very difficult to live with.

The Pentagon has threatened to court martial soldiers who share their faith. This includes military chaplains.[21]

There are some anti-Christian activists who are making life difficult for Christians. For example, a U.S. military chaplain was reprimanded for sharing how his Christian faith enabled him overcome depression. This was during a workshop to help prevent suicide, so what he shared should have helped some soldiers.[22] I seriously doubt if a Wiccan would would have been reprimanded for saying that mind-altering New Age techniques had helped him overcome depression.

A U.S. Marine was court martialed and given a dishonorable discharge because she refused to remove the phrase "No weapon formed against me shall prosper" from her computer.[23] Somebody who doesn't like Christianity knew enough about Scripture to recognize that this was a slightly changed portion of Isaiah 54:17. That text was highly appropriate for a Marine, because their lives are in danger.

I seriously doubt if anybody would have reprimanded a Muslim for having something from the Koran on their computer. The policy seems to be to appease Muslims and attack Christians.

On March 21, 2014, the Family Research Council published a report titled *A Clear and Present Danger: The Threat to Religious Liberty in the Military*. It is 21 pages long and very thoroughly documented. You can get a free PDF file of it online.[24]

There have been some cases where American Christians have been murdered because of their faith.

On September 15, 1999, there was a rally at Wedgewood Baptist Church in Fort Worth, Texas. A gunman entered the church and methodically shot Christians who were attending the service, and then shot himself. Seven people died and others were critically wounded. The gunman was shouting, cursing Christianity, and cursing the Christians for believing it. The FBI found anti-Christian writings in his home.[25]

However, in spite of this evidence, when CBS and CNN reported the shooting, they were "unable to assign any motive to the shooter."[26] Why? Because it is not politically correct to portray Christians as being persecuted. The mainstream media avoids such stories, or else covers them in ways that omit or deny the element of persecution.

I found out about that 20 years ago when I learned that Christians in Sudan were being slaughtered by Muslims. I contacted every newspaper I knew to tell them about it. None of them responded, with one exception. One reporter told me, "I wish I could write about it." So evidently he wanted to cover the story, but was not allowed to.

On April 20, 1999, two students at Columbine High School in Littleton, Colorado shot and killed 12 of their classmates and a teacher, and wounded 23 other people. They also killed themselves. They asked three Christian girls if they believed in God, and killed them when they said "Yes." The girls were Cassie Bernall, Rachel Scott, and Valeen Schnurr. Rachel had shared her Christian faith with the boys several weeks earlier. (Some classmates overheard the conversation.) The boys made a video in which they cursed Jesus Christ and cursed Christians. They singled Rachel Scott out for an insulting tirade, mocking her by name.[27]

I read about the shootings in the newspaper, but those reports didn't mention the element of persecuting Christian students. It took me years to find out about that, and I got the information from a story on a Christian website about Rachel Scott's father. I never heard anything about it from the mainstream media. Did you?

Chapter 2

Brainwashing Christians

In the first chapter, I told you about Jack Phillips, the owner of Masterpiece Cake Shop in Denver, Colorado. He was threatened with fines and possibly prison because he refused to bake a wedding cake for a homosexual couple. He said that he would rather go to prison than compromise his faith and his moral convictions.

He was able to avoid prison and the fines by deciding to never bake any more wedding cakes again. He can't be accused of discriminating if nobody gets his wedding cakes.

That keeps him out of prison, but it make it much more difficult for him to earn a livelihood. In addition, wedding cakes are his specialty and his passion, a form of artistic expression. He has a gift for doing them beautifully, and he loves making them.

This case has taken another turn which is very disturbing. The Colorado Civil Rights Commission has ordered Phillips and all of his staff (which includes his 87-year-old Christian mother) to submit to a regimen of "sensitivity training." This is to make sure that Phillips and the people working for him all agree with the commission's interpretation of Colorado's non-discrimination statute. In other words, they are trying to force Phillips and his staff to believe that it is right and proper for them to bake wedding cakes for homosexual couples.[1]

When the judge ordered him to bake wedding cakes for homosexual couples, Phillips said that, if necessary, he would be willing to go to prison because of his convictions. He said:

"That violates my First Amendment speech… and my duty as a Christian abiding by my Savior."

"I'm not giving up my faith for anything. It's too high a price to pay." [2]

Phillips has been represented by Alliance Defending Freedom (ADF), which is a conservative advocacy group. Nicolle Martin of ADF said:

"Colorado has no business forcing Jack to abandon deeply held convictions… which are protected by the First Amendment, **so the state can impose a new, government-approved belief system upon him**." (Emphasis added) [3]

ADF's Senior Vice President of Legal Services is Kristen Waggoner. She said:

"If the government can take away our First Amendment freedoms, there is no other thing it can't take away." [4]

Lee Duigon has an article about this titled "When the State Owns Your Soul." He begins it by saying:

"Sometimes violence, even murder, isn't the worst thing you can do to a fellow human being. Stealing his soul, taking over the management of his conscience and his mind—those are worse." [5]

This appears to be precisely what the Colorado Civil Rights Commission is attempting to do to Phillips, his elderly mother, and his employees. It also sets a precedent that is probably intended to intimidate other Christian businessmen.

In addition, if they can force Christians to act against their conscience and convictions, then they can do similar things to other groups of people. For example, could black businessmen be required to provide services for KKK functions? Could Jewish businessmen be required to provide services for the Muslim Brotherhood or other anti-Semitic groups?

Phillips and his mother will never agree with the judge's interpretation of Colorado's non-discrimination statute. They will insist that they have a right and a duty to act according to their conscience, which is guided by their Christian faith and by statements in the Bible.

Does this mean that Colorado will require them to keep on taking "sensitivity training" for the rest of their lives, because they have not been "rehabilitated" from their religious beliefs?

Whether or not the state of Colorado winds up trying to push it that far, this is a serious issue. It is about brainwashing. It is about denying freedom of religion and freedom of conscience.

The New York State Division of Human Rights is doing the same thing to the Giffords, who are Christian farmers in Schaghticoke, New York. In addition to farming, they also open their home for weddings and receptions, and they refused to do it for a lesbian couple who wanted to get married there. The state of New York is forcing the Giffords and their staff to take "re-education" classes in order to change their religious and moral convictions.[6]

Since this is happening in two different states, within a few months, it looks as if we are likely to see more cases like these. This could become a national trend.

I know a pastor who for years has been saying that at some point, we are going to have to choose whether to worship God or Caesar (i.e., the state). Right now, the state of Colorado is attempting to force this baker and his employees to worship Caesar—to allow the state to override their conscience and their religious convictions.

That is what Hitler tried to do to the Germans, and what Marx and Stalin tried to do to the Russians. As Dietrich Bonhoeffer said, Hitler wanted to be the conscience of the people. He wanted to put himself in the place of God.

As Christians we must be determined to be faithful to God, and to live Biblically, and to follow our conscience, no matter what it costs. We cannot afford to compromise. There is too much at stake:

> "For what is a man profited, if he shall gain the whole world, and lose his own soul? or what shall a man give in exchange for his soul?" (Matthew 16:26)

Chapter 3

Thought Police In Colleges

Some universities in the United States are subjecting their students to a form of mind control that includes redefining words. The following quotation from L. Ron Hubbard (the founder of Scientology) describes the procedure for doing this:

> "The way to redefine a word is to get the new definition repeated as often as possible... A consistent, repeated effort is the key to any success with this technique of propaganda." (L. Ron Hubbard)[1]

A quotation from the University of Delaware demonstrates how they are applying these principles:

> "A racist is one who is both privileged and socialized on the basis of race by a white supremacist (racist) system. The term applies to **all** white people... living in the United States" (The University of Delaware, emphasis added)[2]

The University of Delaware has about 7,000 students living on campus. It requires all of these students "to adopt highly specific university-approved views on issues ranging from politics to race, sexuality, sociology, moral philosophy and environmentalism." These students are "pressured or even required" to make statements that comply with the school's views.[3]

Being quiet about their beliefs isn't enough to keep students out of trouble. They are interviewed, one-on-one, with intrusive questions. If students fail to give politically correct answers, then a report is written about them, and the students are subjected to "treatment," namely compulsory re-education.

This is a state university, which means that it is supported by taxes. Therefore, people who would be appalled by such things are required by law to support them financially.

The Foundation for Individual Rights in Education (FIRE) has produced a video about this brainwashing. In interviews with students and professors, it shows how the university's Office of Residence Life used a variety of methods to "coerce students to change their thoughts, values, attitudes, beliefs, and habits" so that they would "conform to a highly specified social, environmental, and political agenda." [4]

One of the university's views is that all whites of European descent are, by definition, racists. That would include William Wilberforce, a white Englishman who spent his life working for the abolition of slavery.[5]

Is this hard to believe? Then read these current definitions from the University of Delaware Office of Residence Life Diversity Facilitation Training:

"**A RACIST**: [A]ll white people... By this definition, people of color cannot be racists, because as peoples within the U.S. system, they do not have the power to back up their prejudices" (page 3)

"**A NON-RACIST**: A non-term. The term was created by whites to deny responsibility for systemic racism" (page 3)

The "racist" label would apply to James Reeb, because he was a white American man. He was beaten to death by segregationists on March 11, 1965, because he participated in Rev. Dr. Martin Luther King Jr.'s march for civil rights in Selma, Alabama.[6]

It would also include my friend Sheila, a white woman who also participated in that civil rights march in Selma. Although timid by nature, Sheila could be strong when it came to standing up for what she believed in. She risked her life to participate in that march, and she had to face police dogs and cattle prods. But the University of Delaware says that Sheila is a racist because she is white.

It would also include white couples who adopt black children. And it would include whites who marry blacks. According to the university, these people are, by definition, racists—no matter how they behave, and no matter what they believe.

So according to the University of Delaware, "racism" has little or nothing to do with behavior, beliefs, and motives. It is all about the university's philosophy and ideology. What men and women actually think, and how they actually behave, is considered to be irrelevant.

There was strong resistance to this program at the University of Delaware. As a result, it was discontinued in October 2007.[7] But in May 2008, the program was revived. And it still has the same definition of racism.[8]

The University of Minnesota has proposed a similar program. It apparently intends to change its admissions process in order to screen out potential students who have "wrong" beliefs and values. Present students whose beliefs don't conform to the university's ideology, and who do not change their beliefs as a result of mandatory re-education, would not be able to get degrees. In other words, after successfully completing their studies, they would be refused the degree that they earned because of their personal beliefs.[9]

This program of indoctrination is especially aimed at future teachers. The Teacher Education Redesign Initiative is a group whose objective is to "change the way future teachers are trained" at the University of Minnesota. It requires teachers to embrace (and teach) its worldview, which sees America as being "an oppressive hellhole: racist, sexist and homophobic." [10]

Many American colleges are indoctrinating students instead of educating them. This widespread problem is documented in

Jim Nelson Black's book *Freefall of the American University: How Our Colleges Are Corrupting the Minds and Morals of the Next Generation* (Thomas Nelson, 2004).

This process involves coercion, mind control, and the unconstitutional lack of free speech and freedom of conscience. It also involves "service learning"—sending students into troubled neighborhoods where they are trained to justify immorality and despise traditional values. What does this do to the ability of students to think logically and to deal with objective facts?

Replacing real education with indoctrination creates a generation of students whose beliefs and behavior are ruled by propaganda and feelings instead of facts and logical thinking. These victims of contemporary brainwashing can easily be manipulated by clever slogans, clever music, and clever TV ads. This is a perfect set-up for power-hungry politicians.

Back in the fifties, countless Western prisoners-of-war faced Communist brainwashing in Asia and the Soviet Union. Only those prisoners whose faith and values were anchored in unwavering truth were able to resist the disorienting assaults on their minds. Genuine Christians demonstrated a strong spiritual resistance that baffled Communist change agents and even converted guards.

Never has it been more important to stand firm in God's Word, train our children to reject compromise, and stand together in God-given strength as we face a world that hates our values and mocks our God!

> "What shall we then say to these things? If God be for us, who can be against us?" (Romans 8:31)

Chapter 4

Teaching Kids To Be Sociopaths

In Chapter 1 ("Understanding the Times") I told how some humanists are trying to destroy people's ability to tell the difference between right and wrong. In addition, brainwashing techniques are being used on school children in order to change their moral values. What are the results of such things in real life?

Here is one example. It involves black college students, but it has absolutely nothing to do with racism. I was a civil rights activist back in the days of Dr. Martin Luther King, Jr., and I have a friend who risked her life to march with him in Selma, Alabama. These are facts that show something about what our education system and popular entertainment have done to many of our young people, regardless of race.

In April 2013, there was a race riot in Virginia Beach. There was widespread violence and destruction by black college students who were "having fun." This involved forty thousand college students. That is a huge number of people. It's like a full-fledged invasion.[1]

Their "fun" included destroying a small family business that had taken a lifetime to build. It was the kind of small place that gets "regulars," where people know each other.

That "fun" also resulted in three stabbings, three shootings, and numerous beatings—one so severe that it resulted in bleeding in the brain. These college students were terrifying people "for fun." All of the victims were white, and all of the perpetrators were black.

These were not gang kids. And they were not poor, oppressed, deprived, inner city kids. These were college students. They had enough education and enough money to be able to go to college.

The destruction and violence wasn't based on anger due to some kind of Rodney King incident or anything like that. It was just a bunch of college kids "having fun."

This reminds me of the video of college students having "fun" at a birthday party by playing a game called "abortion battles." Pairs of boys put balloons underneath their shirts, pretending to be pregnant. They attacked each other's bellies with forks, trying to pop those balloons. And the party crowd was laughing and cheering them on, yelling things like, "Kill that baby!" These were college students, mostly white, and girls as much as boys. (You can see a video of this on YouTube.) [2]

It also reminds me of some kids who gang raped a girl. Then they laughed and said things like, "She is **so** raped!" They also urinated on that girl, and bragged about it, laughing as they did. (You can see a video of their bragging on YouTube.) [3]

It also reminds me of something that happened back in the days when I was a temporary secretary, going from place to place. In one office, I worked with a young woman who cheerfully told me that she had deliberately gotten pregnant in order to see if she was able to. Then she had an abortion, because she didn't want to have a baby. She deliberately murdered a baby in order to find out if she was fertile.

She told me about this cheerfully and pleasantly, as part of light conversation, as if what she had done was normal behavior. Here again, we are not talking about some poor, disadvantaged, uneducated person. This was a secretary—a professional with education and special training.

For years, our public schools been promoting "values clarification" and teaching kids that there are no moral absolutes. That objective truth does not exist. That there is no such thing as objective right and wrong. The behavior that I described above is the fruit of that teaching.

The definition of being "criminally insane" is being unable to tell the difference between right and wrong. So we are literally teaching school kids to become criminally insane. Or to put it another way, we are teaching them to become sociopaths.

There is a TV channel called Nickelodeon. Years ago, it had reruns of good old-fashioned, clean-cut shows like "Leave it to Beaver." Parents believed that their kids could safely watch this channel because of the shows that it carried. However, between the segments of the shows, they had quick skits showing children with total disrespect for their parents, and things like that. Perhaps you could call those "commercials for a spirit of lawlessness."

They also had a game show. I saw one episode of it. They took two teams of school kids, and put them in rooms (nice rooms, with nice things in them). The aim of the game was to totally trash the rooms as quickly and as thoroughly as they could. There was upbeat music playing while they did it, and the audience was laughing and cheering. The team that trashed their room the fastest won a prize.

That game was teaching those kids to do exactly what those college students did to that family business in Virginia Beach. And it was teaching that lesson to children in nice homes, in nice neighborhoods, all over America.

For these kids, the people they are hurting don't seem like real people to them. They see them as being just props on their stage—objects to be used, or characters in a video game that they are playing. These young people are acting like sociopaths. And our public schools have taught them to be that way. So have Hollywood and the music industry.

To that mix, add the fact that many colleges today are teaching that, by definition, every white person is a racist, and that racism doesn't depend on what people say, or what they do, or how they think. According to those colleges, just having white skin, by definition, makes people racists. (See Chapter 3, "Thought Police In Colleges.") Therefore, the teachings of those colleges encouraged those black college students to attack, terrify, and vandalize white people in Virginia Beach.

We know that the Nazis and the Communists did things that were cruel and destructive. Some of them were overtly evil people, and they knew exactly what they were doing. However, for many of them, that was not their original intention. They had been taught that what they were doing would lead to a utopia, to a better world for themselves and for their children. They saw themselves as doing something that was necessary in order to bring about the utopia that they longed for. Hard-core communists refer to such people as "useful idiots."

Because they had a conscience, the "useful idiots" had to be deceived in order to get them to do bad things. It took a lot of clever propaganda, shameless lying, and brainwashing techniques in order to get them to the point where they would call evil good, and call good evil, and act accordingly. They were taught that what they were doing would lead to a "greater good," to a better world. Of course, their thinking was twisted. But because they had been deceived, they thought that they were doing the right thing.

What we are seeing here in America has gone even further down the slippery slope. These kids don't have to think that mayhem is for the purpose of creating a "greater good." They will do it just to "have fun"—as if it's just a video game.

Violent video games that they play keep reinforcing that. So does the violent rap music, or demonic rock music, that they keep pumping into their heads. And so do MTV's music videos.

Years ago, I once saw one of those MTV music videos when I was visiting somebody in the hospital. He turned off the sound, but I saw an incredible amount of violence and death and occultism, all mixed in with sex. Of course, that associates death and violence with sexual pleasure. It was unspeakably depraved.

Kids like these seem to have no conscience at all. They have become sociopaths. And these college students will become leaders in society because of their education.

We didn't need to have a Babylonian invasion in order to destroy America. We are doing it to ourselves, from within. And the "cultural Christians" in this nation are allowing it to happen, right under their noses.

As in the days of Elijah, God has a faithful remnant. And He can use even this mess for His glory. He can use it to wake some people up, and make them realize that they need God. They cannot make it on their own. They desperately need God. Once people understand that, then they will turn to God.

As in the days of the early church (which suffered horrible persecution by the Romans), the true church will grow and get stronger. True Christians will become more serious about God, and more devoted to Him and to their brothers and sisters in Christ. What the enemy means for evil, God will use for good.

We are heading for hard times. But individuals who love God will come through the refiner's fire as pure gold. Look at Dietrich Bonhoeffer and Corrie ten Boom.

Chapter 5

A Biblical Warning For America

"If my people, which are called by my name, shall humble themselves, and pray, and seek my face, and turn from their wicked ways; then will I hear from heaven, and will forgive their sin, and will heal their land." (2 Chronicles 7:14)

The Book of Judges shows a gradual process by which the Israelites (God's chosen people) turned away from God in stages, to follow "other gods" (the gods of the Canaanites and other pagans).

These stages are not limited to the Israelites. They also apply to Christians, because we are also God's people. Therefore, we should learn from what happened to the Israelites so that we won't have to go through the suffering that they endured. Here are the stages:

Stage 1. Peace and Prosperity

God blessed His people with peace and prosperity, because He loves them. All seemed to be going well for them. They were grateful, and they loved and served God.

Stage 2. Apathy and Compromise

After a while, the people took God's gifts for granted, and they forgot Him. They served Him apathetically, or else they neglected Him altogether. They found reasons for no longer following God:

"But this thing commanded I them, saying, Obey my voice, and I will be your God, and ye shall be my people: and walk ye in all the ways that I have commanded you, that it may be well unto you. But they hearkened not, nor inclined their ear, but walked in the counsels and in the imagination of their evil heart, and went backward, and not forward." (Jeremiah 7:23-24)

The next chapter ("Heading Towards Dictatorship") shows how this is happening here in America, and how it happened in Germany before Hitler came to power. There are a number of parallels that are quite troubling.

Stage 3. Rebellion and Paganism

The people turned to other gods for strength and help. The Bible calls that spiritual prostitution. We see this analogy very clearly in the book of Hosea, where God compares Israel to a faithless wife who leaves her husband and runs after other men. The Bible says:

"And yet they would not hearken unto their judges, but they went a whoring after other gods, and bowed themselves unto them" (Judges 2:17)

God warned them that because they turned away from Him, He would no longer protect them:

"The Zidonians also, and the Amalekites, and the Maonites, did oppress you; and ye cried to me, and I delivered you out of their hand. Yet ye have forsaken me, and served other gods: wherefore I will deliver you no more. Go and cry unto the gods which ye have chosen; let them deliver you in the time of your tribulation." (Judges 10:12-14)

Stage 4. Famine, War, Plagues and Slavery

God allowed bad things to happen to His people. They went through great suffering:

> "Hear, O earth: behold, I will bring evil upon this people, even the fruit of their thoughts, because they have not hearkened unto my words, nor to my law, but rejected it." (Jeremiah 6:19)

The Israelites were conquered by outsiders. However, people can also be conquered from within. The German people elected Hitler. Then he cleverly undermined the freedom of the people and became a full-fledged dictator. He did it incrementally, in stages, and managed to make each stage seem to be reasonable. By the time the people realized what was happening, it was too late.

Stage 5. Confession and Repentance

God showed the people the inadequacy of their own resources, and the fact that pagan gods would not take care of them. They discovered that they needed God, and they needed to be right with Him. They finally repented and confessed their sins:

> "O Lord, to us belongeth confusion of face, to our kings, to our princes, and to our fathers, because we have sinned against thee. To the Lord our God belong mercies and forgivenesses, though we have rebelled against him; Neither have we obeyed the voice of the Lord our God, to walk in his laws, which he set before us by his servants the prophets... O my God, incline thine ear, and hear; open thine eyes, and behold our desolations, and the city which is called by thy name: for we do not present our supplications before thee for our righteousnesses, but for

thy great mercies. O Lord, hear; O Lord, forgive; O Lord, hearken and do; defer not, for thine own sake, O my God: for thy city and thy people are called by thy name." (Daniel 9:8-10, 18-19)

Stage 6. God Hears, Saves and Restores

God blesses His people with peace. He protects them and prospers them—as long as they follow Him.

Where does the United States fit in this cycle? There are still some Christians who believe the Bible and take God seriously and try to live Biblically. Unfortunately, they are a minority.

Many people go to church for social or cultural reasons, rather than devotion to God. And many pastors preach a watered-down Gospel, because they want their listeners to feel good, so that more people will come, and their church will grow big and be successful in worldly terms.

Some pastors deny foundational Christian doctrines, and some bring New Age teachings and practices into their churches. This is described in *A Time of Departing* by Ray Yungen, and *Pagans in the Pews* by Peter Jones. Randy England's book *The Unicorn in the Sanctuary* tells how the New Age has impacted the Catholic Church.

That is the second stage: apathy and compromise.

In America, humanism can serve as a bridge between Biblical faith and paganism. First, people turn to men as their source of authority, rather than the Bible. Having done that, it is then easier for them to turn to pagan gods. Or, to put it another way, first they make a god out of man, and then they turn to more traditional pagan gods:

"Thus saith the Lord; Cursed be the man that trusteth in man, and maketh flesh his arm, and whose heart departeth from the Lord." (Jeremiah 17:5)

The New Age movement is another bridge between Biblical faith and paganism. First, people get into New Age things. Then from there, they can get into overt paganism. (The New Age movement is pagan, but it is dressed up in modern vocabulary and imagery, so it isn't obvious.)

Pagan goddess worship has gotten into many mainline churches. In addition, it is being taught in public schools, universities, and nursing schools. It is also being promoted by Hollywood, the music industry, and the media. In addition, practical witchcraft is being taught in some public schools.

According to the Bible, pagan gods and goddesses are demons:

"But I say, that the things which the Gentiles sacrifice, they sacrifice to devils, and not to God: and I would not that ye should have fellowship with devils." (1 Corinthians 10:20)

Wiccan beliefs and practices are getting into mainline denominations. For example, two Methodist clergywomen participated in a croning ritual (a witchcraft initiation ritual). They both wrote articles praising their experience in *Wellsprings*, a journal for Methodist clergywomen. When contacted by *Insight on the News*, both women confirmed their participation in the croning ritual, and said that their bishop (a woman) had also participated. When the bishop was contacted, she said that she "witnessed many croning rituals." [1]

That is the third stage: rebellion and paganism.

To get some idea of the degree to which paganism is taking over our society, look at how far we have fallen morally. Pagan morals are directly opposed to Biblical morality. Our movies and

TV and other entertainment often promote pagan values, and many Christians watch it.

The Canaanites had temple prostitutes, and they were men as well as women, and children as well as adults. As a result, when the Israelites turned to worshiping Canaanite gods, they became promiscuous, they practiced homosexuality, and they had sex with children. In addition, they also killed babies, because some of the Canaanite gods (such as Molech) required that they sacrifice their babies.

How far has America fallen into paganism? And what are the potential consequences, according to the cycle that is described in the Book of Judges?

In 1950, most people were virgins when they were married. But now that has become rare because sex before marriage has become the norm.

I never even heard of homosexuality until the 1960s, when I befriended a girl in college who turned out to be bisexual. These days, some children are hearing about homosexuality in kindergarten in our public schools. And some school kids are being forced to act like homosexuals. For example, in one school, girls 13 and 14 years old were told by their teacher to ask other girls for a lesbian kiss.[2]

Today, children are becoming sexually active at incredibly young ages. For example, two five-year-old children in kindergarten had sex in their classroom's bathroom.[3] Kids in public schools are having sex in the hallways, on the stairs, and even in classrooms.[4] (To see some other ways in which many young people have lost their moral compass, see Chapter 4, "Teaching Kids to be Sociopaths.")

You may think, "Well, at least we don't sacrifice babies to pagan gods." True, but we have killed 55 million babies through abortion.[5] In addition, a woman who is both a pagan and a psychologist wrote a book titled *The Sacrament of Abortion*. She calls abortion "a sacred act" that is a sacrifice to the goddess Artemis (also known as Diana).[6]

What about adults having sex with children? Well, some psychologists and academicians are trying to normalize pedophilia. Instead of protecting children from sexual predators, they want to be sensitive to the feelings and sexual orientation of pedophiles, which they have given a name that sounds nicer. They call them "minor-attracted persons."[7]

Another indication of how pagan we have become is the fact that occultism is becoming mainstream. Witchcraft, sorcery, fortune telling, and consulting the dead (necromancy) are strictly forbidden in the Bible. But they have become commonplace. According to a study done in 2006, three out of four teenagers have engaged in "psychic or witchcraft-related activity." Many of them participated in seances, tried to cast a spell, or mixed a magic potion.[8]

In the Book of Judges, once the nation of Israel worshiped pagan gods and goddesses (which includes rejecting Biblical morality in favor of pagan moral standards), then they were heading for judgment.

The next thing that happened was famine, war, plagues, and slavery. Could those things happen in America?

In the alternative news I read about the potential for another major war, perhaps even a world war. Food is already more expensive because unusual weather is hurting crops. In addition, bees are dying off, and they are needed to pollinate crops. Some people are afraid that the American dollar will lose its value, resulting is hyperinflation.

The mainstream media often tells us about diseases that have people worried about the possibility of a pandemic. In addition, one out of four teenaged girls in America has at least one sexually transmitted disease.[9]

You may ask, "What about slavery?" Well, if we wind up with a dictatorship, then we could have slave labor. (See Chapter

6, "Heading Towards Dictatorship.") The Nazis had slave labor in their concentration camps. The Russians, Chinese, and North Koreans have it in their labor camps today.

Modern America has not seen famine or plagues, and we have never lost a war. And I hope that such things will never happen to us. However, we are not immune to them.

Of course, God could protect us from all of that—if we repent and turn back to Him:

> "If my people, which are called by my name, shall humble themselves, and pray, and seek my face, and turn from their wicked ways; then will I hear from heaven, and will forgive their sin, and will heal their land." (2 Chronicles 7:14)

We have some good, solid Christians in America. However, there were also some faithful Israelites during the time of the Babylonian captivity. Daniel was a Godly man, but he had to go into captivity along with his people. And so did Shadrach and Mesach and Abednego. They suffered a lot because of the sins of their countrymen. The problem is that so much of Israel had abandoned God and turned away to pagan gods. The faithful ones like Daniel were small in number compared to those who went "whoring after other gods." (Judges 2:17)

Even if the people all around us turn away from God and Biblical morality, we need to hold on to our integrity. We are doing it for God, not for men. That is part of being faithful to Him.

If our nation suffers because it has turned away from God, then we still need to be faithful to Him. Like Daniel. And like Shadrach, Mesach, and Abednego.

The most important thing is our relationship with God. If we love Him, then He will make ALL things work out for our long-term, eternal good. (Romans 8:28) We are never at the mercy of men or circumstances, because no matter what happens, God can bring good out of it.

Conversely, for those who don't love God, nothing will do them any good. Even if they have a pleasant life here on earth, it won't do them any good in the long term, because when they die, they will wind up in hell.

The bottom line is our relationship with God. Not our circumstances.

In the musical *Fiddler on the Roof,* Reb Tevye sings a song to his wife: "Do You Love Me?" Well, God has been asking us that question all through history. Every single person who was ever born has to answer that question. And they don't just answer it in words. They answer it by how they live, and how they relate to God.

Unfortunately, most people reject God. He created them, and He loves them, but they reject Him. Something else is more important to them. Something else takes first place instead of God. The Bible calls that idolatry. Jesus told us:

> "Enter ye in at the strait gate: for wide is the gate, and broad is the way, that leadeth to destruction, and many there be which go in thereat: Because strait is the gate, and narrow is the way, which leadeth unto life, and few there be that find it." (Matthew 7:13-14)

God has suffered so much unrequited love. That's all the more reason for us to love Him. He created us so that we could love Him. So let's love Him deeply, and faithfully, and consistently. And let's do whatever we can to help others love Him.

Worldviews

The worldview of Christians should be based on the Bible, and on their understanding of, and relationship with, the Lord Jesus

Christ. However, we live in a world with many other beliefs, values, and ways of thinking.

Christians have a very different worldview from that of pagans and New Agers. They have different approaches to theology, philosophy, psychology, morality, child rearing, and other areas of life.

We need to respect people with other worldviews, because all men and women are created in the image of God. (Genesis 1:26-28) In addition, Jesus died for all of us, in order to make it possible for us to become rightly related to God and go to Heaven. If Jesus thinks that the people we disagree with are worth dying for, then we should respect them and love them for His sake.

We can love and respect people without agreeing with them. We can even love them when they do things that are quite hurtful. For example, when Betsy ten Boom was in a Nazi concentration camp, she forgave the Nazi guards who did cruel things to her, and she prayed for them.

After the war was over, Betsy's sister Corrie encountered one of those guards. He had become a Christian after the war. Corrie was able to love him, in spite of the cruel things that he had done in the past. They hugged each other and wept.

When Corrie heard that the man who had betrayed her family was in prison and was going to be executed, she wrote him a letter telling him that she forgave him, and telling him about the love and forgiveness of Jesus. That man became a Christian before he was killed, and Corrie rejoiced because of it.

Now respecting people with other worldviews does **not** mean that we should compromise our own Christian worldview. All worldviews are **not** equal, and all "paths" do **not** lead to the same place.

For example, if the atheists are right, then when we die, we will all stop existing. If the New Agers and Hindus are right, then when we die, we will be reincarnated. If the Christians are right, then when we die we will go to Heaven or we will go to hell.

They cannot all be right, because the end results are so radically different.

As Christians, we need to stand firm in our faith, and not apologize for our Biblical worldview. We will be vindicated in eternity. In the meantime, we should show love to people who don't know Jesus as their Lord and Savior. And we should pray for their salvation.

On a practical note, loving people does not necessarily mean that we trust their judgment. If their moral standards are different from ours, then we should not let them babysit our children. And we would be foolish to be business partners with them. Also, we should not get romantically involved with them. The Bible warns us not to be "unequally yoked." (2 Corinthians 6:14)

We need to protect our children from the influence of such people. And we need to be careful not to allow our faith or our morals to become compromised by them.

Attempts to Blend Christianity with Other Religions

There are a number of attempts to blend Christianity with other religions on a world-wide scale. You can read about them in "Unveiling the Global Interfaith Agenda." [10]

There are also other attempts to merge Christianity with different religions. For example, Chrislam tries to combine Christianity with Islam. There are some occultists who claim to be Christian witches (i.e., combining Christianity with Wicca). Some pagans attempt to mix Christianity with Hinduism, and with Buddhism, and with Shamanism. (A shaman is a Native American medicine man.) Some people claim to be Christian witch doctors or Christian sorcerers. You can buy a book about "Christian" Voodoo.[11]

In 2009, Barna did a survey of worldviews among American adults. Only nineteen percent of "born again Christians" in the United States have a Biblical worldview. That is less than one out of five. Among the population as a whole, nine percent of adults have a Biblical worldview. ***Among American adults who are between the ages of 18 and 23, less than one-half of one percent have a Biblical worldview.***[12]

Nominal Christians are people who are Christians in name only. They call themselves Christians, but they really aren't. They ignore, or openly deny, foundational Christian doctrines, and they don't try to live the way that God told us to live, as described in the Bible. Such people can fit in with other religions. However, real Christians aren't able to do that. Biblical Christianity cannot mix with other religions.

To compare it to something physical in everyday life, you cannot mix oil and water. Because of their very nature, they just don't mix. You can put them in a glass jar and shake them until they seem to be blended, but then they will separate and the oil will rise to the top of the jar.

To carry that analogy further, if you add an emulsifier, then they can mix. It goes against their nature, but the emulsifier bridges that gap. In real life, Christians who are under severe pressure (such as the fear of prison or torture or death) may go against their nature and try to blend in with whatever is politically correct. That happened in Nazi Germany. I've seen pictures of church altars with swasticas on them. However, Jesus warned us not to make such compromises:

> "Whosoever therefore shall confess me before men, him will I confess also before my Father which is in heaven. But whosoever shall deny me before men, him will I also deny before my Father which is in heaven." (Matthew 10:32-33)

These days, it is not politically correct to be "exclusive" by claiming that Jesus Christ is the only way to salvation. However, we need to be Biblically correct rather than politically correct.

The antidote to the fear of men is the fear of God. Jesus warned us:

> "And fear not them which kill the body, but are not able to kill the soul: but rather fear him which is able to destroy both soul and body in hell." (Matthew 10:28)

Jesus made it very clear that He is the **only** way to be right with God the Father. There is no other source of salvation. He said:

> "I am the way, the truth, and the life: no man cometh unto the Father, but by me." (John 14:6)

> "I am the door: by me if any man enter in, he shall be saved, and shall go in and out, and find pasture. The thief cometh not, but for to steal, and to kill, and to destroy: I am come that they might have life, and that they might have it more abundantly. I am the good shepherd: the good shepherd giveth his life for the sheep." (John 10:7-11)

My Hope is Built on Nothing Less
(by Edward Mote, 1797-1874, *public domain*)

My hope is built on nothing less
Than Jesus' blood and righteousness;
I dare not trust the sweetest frame,
But wholly lean on Jesus' name.
On Christ, the solid Rock, I stand;
All other ground is sinking sand.

When darkness veils His lovely face,
I rest on His unchanging grace;
In every high and stormy gale
My anchor holds within the veil.
On Christ, the solid Rock, I stand;
All other ground is sinking sand.

His oath, His covenant, and blood
Support me in the whelming flood;
When every earthly prop gives way,
He then is all my Hope and Stay.
On Christ, the solid Rock, I stand;
All other ground is sinking sand.

When He shall come with trumpet sound,
Oh, may I then in Him be found,
Clothed in His righteousness alone,
Faultless to stand before the throne!
On Christ, the solid Rock, I stand;
All other ground is sinking sand.

Chapter 6

Heading Towards Dictatorship

History shows us that as free nations become complacent, they become vulnerable to manipulation. Most dictatorships rise gradually—a step at a time. Smooth-talking politicians make each incremental step seem reasonable, because the masses are blind to the tides of change.

We have been warned over and over. But sadly, a time comes when the wisdom of the watchmen is no longer heeded:

> "Eternal vigilance is the price of liberty." (Wendell Phillips)

> "Giving leaders enough power to create 'social justice' is giving them enough power to destroy all justice, all freedom, and all human dignity." (Thomas Sowell)

> "Those who cannot remember the past are condemned to repeat it." (George Santayana)

> "The greater the power, the more dangerous the abuse." (Edmund Burke)

Austria illustrates the power of gradualism. In 1933, it was a free nation. In 1934, its government began to centralize its power and welcome the influence of Nazi sympathizers. By 1938, it had become a Nazi dictatorship.

The downward slide began with one crisis after another. A third of the people were out of work, inflation rose to 25%, and political turmoil caused civil unrest. People longed for a leader to rescue them. Adolf Hitler campaigned in Austria, promising to

Heading Towards Dictatorship

solve their problems if they were annexed to Germany. A persuasive speaker, he gave them hope and won their hearts. The Austrian people voted him in.[1]

Why? How could the Austrians be so blind? The answer is simple: they faced hard times, so they chose to believe Hitler's promises. They didn't see him as we do—brutal, arrogant, narcissistic and ruthlessly ambitious. That image came later, when it was too late to escape his grasp.

In the beginning, Hitler appeared as a caring, charismatic, captivating visionary.[2] His words brought hope of prosperity, and his public image was intentionally shaped with pictures of his smiles, benevolent deeds and warm encounters with children and babies.[3]

After the annexation, new government jobs were created and order was restored. The people were encouraged and hopeful, and—for a short while—the nation prospered. Then it crashed. This transformation is described by Kitty Werthmann, who lived in Austria when it was ruled by the Nazis:[4]

> "Dictatorship did not happen overnight. It was a gradual process starting with national identification cards, which we had to carry with us at all times."

Next came gun registration, followed by attacks on freedom of speech. There were so many informers that people became afraid to say anything political, even when they were in their own homes.

She tells of other changes, including nationalization of education; indoctrination of children; socialized medicine; government control of businesses; and a lack of respect for human life. Before the annexation, most Austrian mothers stayed at home to take care of their children. Under Nazi rule, both parents had to work, so the children were sent to government-run daycare centers.

Gun control came in two stages. First there was gun registration, and then the people were required to give up their guns. Once the people were unarmed, they had no way of defending themselves against the Nazis. After that, political correctness replaced freedom of speech; taxes were increased to eighty percent (four fifths of income); the nation was filled with informers; anybody who spoke against the government was arrested; and the people lived in constant fear.

In Austria, the transformation from freedom to dictatorship was incremental. No nation is immune to such things, including the United States. In fact, America seems to be following some of the same incremental steps toward totalitarianism.

National Identification Cards

In 2005, Congress passed the Real ID Act. This, in effect, would turn drivers' licenses into a national ID card. However, the law is controversial, and 17 states have passed legislation or resolutions opposing compliance with it. [5]

Congress eventually repealed the law. However, there are ongoing attempts to do things that are similar, but not as comprehensive. According to an article dated March 28, 2013, Senators Chuck Schumer and Lindsey Graham are determined to get a biometric national ID card required for everybody who is employed. And this is so important that they met with President Obama to discuss the matter. [6]

Nationalizing Education and Indoctrinating Young Children

Kitty Werthmann told us how Hitler nationalized the education system. Christian symbols were removed and prayer was banned. Through their government-run child care program, the Nazis would indoctrinate the children with politically correct ideology and absolute loyalty to Hitler. Hitler worship became part of the new structure. The daycare workers were trained in Marxist psychology, not motherly love, for Hitler was fascinated with communist methods of mind control.

Children idolized Hitler and sang his praises. Some American children have been taught to do the same for Obama. I have seen videos of young children singing Obama's praises with adoration, and teenagers singing his praises quite militantly. I have also seen a video of a young boy praying to Obama. (Once such videos become controversial then they tend to disappear from YouTube, so you might have difficulty finding them.)

America is also a nation where prayer is no longer allowed in school, and daycare is common. Obama is centralizing the public schools. His administration is completing a process begun in the nineties during the first Bush administration. A national curriculum with national standards, national tests, and a national database is fast becoming a reality. The goal is to provide "cradle-to-career education for all of America's children." The federal government is encouraging the states to provide children with "early learning experiences from birth through kindergarten entry." [7]

By imposing government education at such a young age, this un-American system exposes Christian children to the worldviews of secular humanism, neo-paganism, and countless other beliefs that clash with home-taught values. It subjects them to anti-Christian peer pressure, and to teachers who are determined to undermine their faith. No wonder children raised in Christian homes from coast to coast are fast rejecting our God and His ways. Meanwhile, churches and youth leaders are bending over backwards to conform to the new values and wants of our youth.

Government schools and the judicial system work hand-in-hand to undermine the faith of Christian children. For example, Amanda is a ten-year-old Christian homeschooler. She is "well liked, social and interactive with her peers, academically promising and intellectually at or superior to grade level." Her homeschool curriculum meets all state standards. Yet, a judge has ordered her to attend public school because of her "vigorous defense of her religious beliefs." The judge wants her to consider "different points of view at a time when she must begin to critically evaluate multiple systems of belief."[8] In other words, he is forcing her into government education in order to challenge her Christian faith.

Buried inside the health care bill is a provision that gives the federal government control over all student loans. As a result, the government can now decide which students are able to go to college. It can also refuse loans for students who want to attend colleges that the government doesn't approve of, thus putting financial pressure on colleges to be politically correct.[9]

New federal regulations would enable the federal government to control the accreditation of all U.S. colleges. According to former U.S. Senator Bill Armstrong, "the Department of Education is attempting to subject every college and university in America—public and private—to political supervision."[10]

Government Control of Health Care and Businesses

Obama's massive health care bill established government control of health care, which is one sixth of the nation's economy. Its regulation will have a devastating effect on the medical profession. Why would bright students want to invest in medical school when the pay would be minimal and medical "murder" would be mandated? My foot doctor told me, "Obama wants to make me retire early." My general practitioner told me, "Let me take care of you while I still can."

The federal government is wielding an increasing degree of control over businesses, both directly and through regulations. Obama's destructive control over Chrysler has been called "another extraordinary intervention into private industry by the federal government." As a result, many car dealerships were closed.[11] According to an attorney who represents some of those dealers, Chrysler closed them because it was "under enormous pressure from the President's automotive task force."[12]

Treating People Like Livestock

Farmers can kill animals that are born sickly or become too old to be productive. Likewise, Hitler talked about getting rid of "useless eaters." In modern America, some "experts" want to dispose of people with a poor "quality of life."

Kitty Werthmann told how the Nazis killed the mentally retarded people in her village. That was a result of Hitler's eugenics program. He was following the unconscionable Darwinian ideals of an evolving, purified human race, and he wanted to produce a Master Race of strong, intelligent Aryans. People he considered to be inferior (including Jews and the mentally retarded) had to be eliminated.[13]

Because of the Holocaust, eugenics was discredited. However, euthanasia (both voluntary and involuntary) is spreading. Voluntary euthanasia is a form of suicide, where patients choose to die—usually with a physician's help. This is legal in Oregon and Washington.[14]

Involuntary euthanasia is based on new, convenient medical standards. In Holland, where thousands of patients have been killed against their will, some elderly people are afraid to go to the hospital.[15] A concerned Belgian citizen warned Western nations to guard themselves against "the encroaching euthanasia agenda."[16]

An influential bioethicist in the Obama administration actively promotes health care rationing.[17] Obama's health care law includes "death panels" with authority to deny life-saving medical care.[18] Once such care has been denied, it becomes unavailable even to patients who would pay the cost themselves.

Gun Control

U.S. Attorney General Eric Holder has a long record of supporting gun control. In a 2008 brief to the Supreme Court, Holder claimed that the Second Amendment does not pose any obstacle to banning guns.[19]

Since the shooting at Sandy Hook, the attempts at gun control have increased in both variety and intensity.

Obama has initiated a back-door approach to gun control by means of an international treaty known as CIFTA. President Clinton signed this treaty in 1997 but the Senate refused to ratify it. Now President Obama is promoting it. According to John Bolton (former U.S. representative of the United Nations):

> "...there's no doubt—as was the case over a decade ago—that the real agenda is the control of domestic arms." [20]

Enforcing Political Correctness

President Obama has co-sponsored a United Nations resolution that calls on countries to criminalize "any advocacy of national, racial or religious hatred that constitutes incitement to discrimination, hostility or violence." Since the President of the United States is backing the resolution, Americans will be expected to abide by it. As a result, this U.N. resolution would take priority over our constitutional right to free speech. In addition, as Robert Spencer said:

> "'Incitement' and 'hatred' are in the eye of the beholder—or more precisely, in the eye of those who make such determinations." [21]

As a result, people in power can silence those who disagree with them by classifying their statements as "hate speech."

In 2008, a Commissioner of the Federal Communications Commission warned that the FCC is likely to attempt to implement regulations that will give the federal government control over the content of radio, TV, and the Internet.[22]

In 2009, a high-ranking official in the FCC called for a "confrontational movement" to increase federal control of the media.[23] He openly expressed admiration for Hugo Chavez' efforts to stifle criticism by seizing control of Venezuela's media.[24]

The Chairman of the FCC is "poised to add the Internet to its portfolio of regulated industries."[25] In other words, the media must be controlled by the government:

> "Mr. Genachowski suggested that government red tape will increase the 'freedom' of online services that have flourished because bureaucratic busybodies have been blocked from tinkering with the Web."[25]

An FCC Commissioner named Michael Copps has proposed a plan: a "public value test" for media. Who will pass that government test? Those who don't will not get their licenses renewed.

> "Copps declared FCC adoption of his Public Values Test would provide an antidote to the current state of affairs by requiring: more diversity... enhanced disclosure of information"[26]

This reminds me of the difference between Russian Communism and Hitler's National Socialism. Stalin ended up with a very poor country. Hitler's socialism allowed for government controlled "free" enterprise, and at first it seemed to succeed. The difference between the two forms of tyrannical socialism was that Stalin's government owned everything, while Hitler controlled everything.

Informers

In 2002, the federal government attempted to recruit four percent of the population as informers. These spies were to include people with access to homes and businesses, such as mailmen, meter readers, cable installers, and telephone repairmen.[27] After a public outcry, this plan was abandoned. However, the attempt to have informants throughout the country is not new. It has continued in various ways, for years.[28]

As part of President Clinton's war on "hate crimes," the Justice Department had a website that encouraged children to report relatives who made a "derogatory comment."[29] Now that Congress has passed the "Hate Crimes" bill, we need to be alert to similar attempts to turn children into informers.

A "smartphone" is a wireless, pocket-sized computer that also functions as a cell phone.[30] It can take pictures.[31] The iPhone is a line of Internet smartphones produced by Apple Computer. People can get "applications" ("apps") for it, enabling them to do a wide variety of things, including GPS navigation and social networking.[32] A person could use their iPhone to take a picture, get the precise location of the place (via GPS), and send the picture and location information to somebody via email, or post it on the Internet.

A new "app" for iPhones enables citizens to spy on one another and report directly to several federal agencies, including the FBI and the Department of Justice.[33] Although this "app" is promoted as a means of preventing terrorism, these spying citizens are also encouraged to report on things such as "environmental negligence" and "discrimination."[34]

The Ability to Arrest People at Will

The President can legally declare a state of national emergency on his own authority without the approval of Congress. There is no legal accountability. Once a national emergency has been declared, the President can "take over all government functions" and "direct all private sector activities" until he declares that the national emergency is over.[35]

A Master Arrest Warrant enables the U.S. Attorney General to have people arrested if he personally considers them to be "dangerous to the public peace and safety." He can keep these people incarcerated indefinitely without legal accountability.[36]

According to a U.S. Congressman, former Rep. Henry Gonzalez, there are detention camps in America. He said that, in the name of stopping terrorism, the President could evoke the military and arrest American citizens and put them in these camps.[37]

If American troops are unwilling or unable to carry out such arrests, then the President can use Canadian troops, thanks to a military agreement called the Civil Assistance Plan.[38] The President can also use troops from the United Nations.[39]

In 2009, a bill in Congress (H.R. 645) required the Department of Homeland Security to establish at least six more detention camps on military installations. It also appears to further expand the president's emergency power.[40] Jerome Corsi observes:

> "We are talking about a slippery slope: camps being prepared to be used in emergencies can easily be used to imprison dissenters." [41]

The bill failed to pass. However, it was introduced again on January 23, 2013 as H.R. 390. It failed to pass, but I suspect that they will try again. Also it might be possible to bypass Congress and do it by means of an executive order.

In addition, there are abandoned indoor shopping malls scattered all over the country. Some people believe that these could be converted into detention centers.

Further Increasing Federal Power

The Obama administration's Financial Reform Bill was signed into law on July 21, 2010. It establishes an Office of Financial Research which would have "unprecedented, real-time access to a wealth of personal and corporate financial data." [42] This new agency would not be accountable to anyone, and it could use coercion to get information.[43]

The Senate has a bill which would give the federal government much more control over our food supply. It threatens to increase food prices and drive many small local suppliers out of business.[44] Even without this new law, Federal agents have already harassed small farms. In April 2010, they invaded a private dairy that doesn't sell to the public.[45]

The Federal Trade Commission and the Federal Communications Commission are discussing ways to regulate what Americans are able to read and hear. These proposed regulations "would apply across the board to print media, radio and television, and the internet." [46]

In July 2, 2008, presidential candidate Obama said that the military is not sufficient for our national security. He said:

"We've got to have a civilian national security force that's just as powerful, just as strong, just as well-funded." [47]

In March 2009, President Obama again discussed the need for a Civilian National Security Force.[48]

One approach to this is via Obama's Health Care law. It establishes a Ready Reserve Corps that would be subject to "involuntary calls to active duty during national emergencies and public health crises." [49] An article giving details about this corps is titled "Obama Just Got His Private Army." [50]

Another approach is the Universal National Service Act. If passed, this bill would require every American (including young mothers) from ages 18 to 42 to spend two years either serving in the military or doing national service as defined by the President.[51] The bill contains some provisions that could be used to promote a globalist agenda.[52]

A National Security Letter (NSL) enables the FBI and other federal agencies to require people to give them information without "probable cause" or judicial oversight. Under the Patriot Act, the NSL includes a "gag order."[53] According to Judge Andrew Napolitano, this makes it a crime for people to speak the truth. He said:

> "If an FBI agent shows up at your house with a self-written search warrant, the agent will tell you, you may not tell anyone about this."[54]

According to Judge Napolitano, if a person whose home was searched in this way was questioned in court about it, under oath, he would not be able to answer truthfully without violating the Patriot Act. In other words, he would have to either commit perjury or else violate the Patriot Act.

Bypassing Congress and Ruling by Executive Regulations

On December 23, 2010, the Department of Interior issued a Secretarial Order giving itself the authority to designate public lands as "Wild Lands." On the same day, the Environmental Protection Agency announced that it will impose carbon emission regulations on power plants and oil refineries. This is "another power grab effectively enacting what Congress had firmly rejected when presented as cap-and-trade legislation."[55]

The *Washington Post* wrote an article about these executive power grabs. It said:

"The move... demonstrated that the Obama administration is prepared to push its environmental agenda through regulation where it has failed on Capitol Hill." [56]

Accuracy in Media called *The Washington Post's* article "matter-of-fact reporting about lawlessness by the federal government." It called this a reflection of the sad state of American journalism, saying:

"There was no hint that this approach is illegal or unconstitutional. The account simply assumes that the Obama Administration can do what it wants, no matter what Congress or the law says." [57]

These administrative power grabs reflect the advice given in a recent report written by the Center for American Progress, which is funded by George Soros. The report is titled "The Power of the President: Recommendations to Advance Progressive Change." [58]

The original health care bill contained mandatory end-of-life counseling. Many saw this as being a slippery slope that could lead to "death panels." Because of the controversy, Congress removed the provision from the bill. But now end-of-life counseling has crept back in through a new Medicare regulation.[59] Once again, the Obama administration has used regulatory fiat to bypass the will of Congress and the American people. Charles Krauthammer said:

"These regulatory power plays make political sense... How better to impose a liberal agenda on a center-right nation than regulatory stealth?" [60]

Inceasing Militarization of the Police

Policemen used to be "peace officers" who served and protected the public. However, the new trend is to become increasingly militarized, including using SWAT teams for minor offenses, and traumatizing families in the process. For example, in 2008, a SWAT team with semi-automatic rifles raided a rural home and food co-op, holding the family (including small children) at gunpoint for hours.[61]

These days, some policemen dress and act like soldiers, complete with military-looking vehicles. You can read about the extent of what is going on, and how this trend developed, in Radley Balko's book *Rise of the Warrior Cop: The Militarization of America's Police Forces*, which was published in July 2013.

Chapter 7

Mainstreaming Occultism

Our nation is inundated with occultism, from cute little Smurfs doing magic in children's cartoons to overtly evil occultists in adult movies. Paganism and occultism (which often go together) seem to be everywhere. They are in popular music, books, movies, TV shows, and video games. They are openly endorsed on tee-shirts and tattoos, in jewelry, in sculptures and pictures, and on bumper stickers.

Many people are fascinated with vampires and zombies and werewolves. There are popular romance novels about normal humans falling in love with such things. One example is the "Twilight" movies, where girls swoon over a handsome vampire.

There is also a fascination with death. One form is "death metal" rock music, and the popularity of skulls and other signs of death on clothing and even in tattoos. A more extreme form of attraction to death is people who like to spend the night at cemeteries, hoping to encounter spirits of the dead.

Such things remind me of a warning that God gave us in the Book of Proverbs:

> "But he that sinneth against me wrongeth his own soul: all they that hate me **love death**." (Proverbs 8:36, emphasis added)

Ancient pagan religions are being revived. There are neo-pagans and modern druids. The Norse god Thor is being worshiped again, and people wear Thor's hammer on chains around their necks, similar to the way that Christians wear crosses. The old Celtic gods and goddesses are being worshiped again, as are ancient Greek and Roman and Babylonian deities.

Witchcraft

In our post-modern world, witchcraft has become so mainstream that it is being taught in universities and nursing schools. Practical witchcraft is also being taught to young children in some of our public schools.

Witchcraft has gotten into some mainline churches. There are ordained female ministers who are also practicing witches at the same time. Two clergywomen who went through a witchcraft initiation ritual were so enthusiastic about their experience that they wrote an article praising it in a publication for clergywomen. Their bishop (a woman) had attended many such rituals, which means that she approves of them. So there is at least one woman bishop who is a practicing witch but claims to be Christian.[1]

Appendix A ("Goddess Worship in America") has some eye-opening information about such things, and it is all thoroughly documented.

In America, Wicca is a tax-exempt religion. It is based on witchcraft, goddess worship, and nature worship. We have Wiccan chaplains in the military and in many prisons. One such chaplain calls herself Rev. Witch.

The soap opera "Charmed" was about three sisters who were good witches. It was so popular that for years people watched the current episodes in the afternoon, and reruns of old episodes in the evening. I learned about this when I was in the hospital, because my roommate was a fan of the show. Although she called herself a Christian, while she was watching one show I heard her say to herself, "I wonder if I have powers."

Sorcery

Somehow "wizard" sounds nicer than "sorcerer," doesn't it? But it's the same thing. In the old days, they were also called alchemists, or those who "practice magic arts."

Sorcery used to be done in secret, by men who hid what they were doing. However, thanks to the popularity of Harry Potter, people have become far more open about it.

When the first Harry Potter movie came out, I searched the Internet for things relating to Hogwarts (his school for wizards). Many of the websites were just entertainment, but some of them featured real live sorcerers who gave practical instructions in sorcery to people who came to those sites.

God Forbids Occultism

Thanks to popular books and movies, many people today believe that there is "white witchcraft" which is done by "good" witches—as opposed to the bad witches. And they also believe that there are "good" wizards (sorcerers).

However, that is not what God says in His Word. God makes it very clear that any kind of occultism is absolutely wrong. He calls it an abomination:

> "There shall not be found among you any one that maketh his son or his daughter to pass through the fire [child sacrifice], or that useth divination, or an observer of times [astrology], or an enchanter [working spells], or a witch [practicing witchcraft or consulting a witch], or a charmer [using charms, amulets and other objects for protection or "good luck"], or a consulter with familiar spirits [doing channeling, or using Ouija boards], or a wizard [sorcery], or a necromancer [someone who contacts the dead, spiritism]. For all that do these things are an abomination unto the Lord." (Deuteronomy 18:10-12)

Many people think that using Ouija boards is just a game. However, if it "works," then that means that they have made contact with a spirit.

Satanism

When it comes to overt evil and blasphemy, satanism is the ultimate. In spite of that, in America, they are a tax-exempt religion that is recognized by the state.

A friend of mine who served in the Air Force had a commanding officer who was openly a satanist. My friend told me that satanists are attracted to the military because satanism is a protected religion there. In addition, satanists can rise in the ranks and get power over other people, and they like to have power.

Some satanists are trying to change their image. For example, a satanist "church" in Oklahoma City rented out the civic center to do a "blasphemy ritual" that was open to the public. This particular ritual was described as being a "parody of the Catholic rite of exorcism." The purpose of the ritual was to cast out God. In other words, they openly hate God and they want to get rid of Him.

This event was advertised, and the group was interviewed by ABC News. The satanic "church" sold tickets to the event.

This satanist group claims to be benign, and to have replaced devil worship with "a religion where god doesn't exist but rituals are used to empower the believer." Their leader said, "We don't kill animals, we don't kill children." [2]

If God doesn't exist, then why would they do an "exorcism" to try to cast Him out? They don't want Him to exist. But He does. And at some level they must know it.

Another attempt to mainstream satanism was to have a Black Mass at Harvard University. The local Catholics protested so much that the ritual was held off campus instead of being done at Harvard. However, since it had received a lot of publicity, I suspect that some Harvard students and local people attended, if only out of curiosity. [3]

In describing this event, Reuters called it a "parody" of the Catholic Mass. That term is misleading. This is not just mocking Catholicism. It is a serious attempt to blaspheme God. The satanists desecrate bread that has been consecrated by a priest. This can be accomplished in two ways. The most common is to steal consecrated hosts from a Catholic Church. But the preferred way is to have an ordained Catholic or Orthodox priest who is also a satanist.

Does this sound impossible? Not really, because people an change. For example, according to Pastor Richard Wurmbrandt, Karl Marx started out as a devout Russian Orthodox and wound up being a satanist. You can read about this in his books *Was Karl Marx A Satanist?* and *Marx & Satan.*

Catholics believe that Jesus Christ is literally present in the consecrated bread and wine. Satanists also believe this, which is why they desecrate the bread and wine. They are trying to hurt and humiliate the Lord Jesus Christ.

Protestants don't believe that doctrine. Therefore, they don't believe that Jesus Christ can be harmed by satanists, or that He needs to be protected from them by men who are loyal to Him.

That issue is beyond the scope of this book. My point is to show the intention of the satanists. The Black Mass is a way of unleashing their hatred for God, and trying to cause Him as much suffering as possible.

There is another significant attempt to mainstream satanism. The Satanic Temple from New York is trying to force Oklahoma to allow them to put a satanic statue in Oklahoma's State Capitol. This statue will be seven feet tall, so that group must have a lot of money.

Some of the height of the statue comes from a throne that the devil is sitting on. The back part of the throne features a huge pentagram that is above the devil's head. The devil has big horns, but because they are in front of the throne, they don't stand out. Because of the throne, you don't see the shape of horns sticking up in the air by themselves.

This statue tries to make the devil look benign. He has a goat's head with horns, but his face isn't nasty. They have softened it. He is sitting on a throne that has a large pentagram, but the pentagram isn't part of him. His bat's wings looks softer than demonic pictures normally do. He is modest, as his body is covered by draped cloth.

There is a little girl on one side of him, and a little boy on the other side of him. The boy seems to be smiling. The devil's lap is about waist high for the sculptured children, so real live children would be able to climb up into his lap and sit there.[4]

The article about this mentions that this is a portrayal of Satan as Baphomet. However, it fails to mention that this is very different from the usual statues or drawing of Baphomet that are intended for the use of fellow occultists. That one is is naked, with the large breasts of a woman. He has a thick pentagram on his forehead. His face is so evil that I wish I had never seen a picture of it. And he has a large phallus sticking up, with two snakes twined around it.

You can find pictures of Baphomet by searching for his name online. However, if you are a visual person, then I don't recommend doing it because it's better not to have seriously evil images get into our heads. Personally I wish that I had never seen this thing because its face is so evil.

The statue that they are trying to put in Oklahoma is an attempt to make something horribly evil appear to be harmless. And to make it appealing to children. One article about this said that the statue is intended to be "interactive with children."

Earlier I mentioned the satanic group that rented out the civic center in Oklahoma City. The group's leader said that they don't kill animals or children. Well, maybe that group doesn't. (But he could have been lying about that.) Whether or not he was telling the truth, there definitely are satanic groups who kill children and animals.

I have a Christian friend who used to be a satanist. According to him, satanists kill animals during their rituals. And some satanists kill people.

I have another Christian friend who is a psychiatric nurse. She has worked with many patients who were victims of satanic ritual abuse. Many of them were raped. Some of them were forced to watch people be murdered as blood sacrifices to the devil. And some of them went through other kinds of horrible experiences.

There is an important book about this kind of thing. It tells about nation-wide child trafficking, satanic ritual murder, and political corruption at high levels, including within the FBI. The book is titled *The Franklin Cover-up: Child Abuse, Satanism, and Murder in Nebraska*. The author is John W. DeCamp, who is an attorney who is representing some of the victims. I'm grateful that the book exists, but I don't recommend reading it unless you have a "need to know." Some things are so evil that it is better not to get them into our heads.

This stuff is for real. But the public relations arm of the satanists is trying to lure people into thinking that satanism is benign and misunderstood. They make satanism appear to be moderate and reasonable—a matter of symbols and pageantry and the empowerment of man, rather than worship of the devil. However, when listening to them, we need to remember that they serve the father of lies. Jesus said:

> "Ye are of your father the devil, and the lusts of your father ye will do. He was a murderer from the beginning, and abode not in the truth, because there is no truth in him. When he speaketh a lie, he speaketh of his own: for **he is a liar, and the father of it**." (John 8:44, emphasis added)

Therefore, why should we believe anything that satanists say? They are openly serving the father of lies.

Smooth-talking satanists can make it look reasonable and benign and fascinating. And then when people are drawn to it, the satanists can spot the individuals who are ready to go "deeper" (i.e., become more overtly evil), and draw them into an inside group that does things that the other people aren't aware of. God warned us:

"Woe unto them that call evil good, and good evil; that put darkness for light, and light for darkness; that put bitter for sweet, and sweet for bitter! Woe unto them that are wise in their own eyes, and prudent in their own sight!" (Isaiah 5:20-21)

People's attitudes and beliefs vary widely. Therefore, I would expect to find "denominations" among satanists, just as there are among Christians. And even within those "denominations," there could be a wide variety of beliefs and practices, just as there are within Christian denominations. For example, the Presbyterian Church USA has voted to accept homosexual marriage. However, there are some smaller, more conservative Presbyterian groups that refuse to accept it.

Such variety can even be found within individual churches. For example, I used to attend a Baptist church whose pastor described himself as being "conservative but not fundamentalist." However, over a period of time we came to realize that he allowed serious heresies to be taught in his church. In addition, some of his sermons suggested that people should be open to such teachings. But he did it in a way that sounded learned and reasonable.

My Bible study group consisted of older people who really believed the Bible. But in that same church, there was a study group that took the teachings of the book *The Shack* very seriously. Instead of refuting it, they embraced it. *The Shack* portrays God as being a woman. It also denies sin and the need for repentance. It portrays God as having a mushy kind of love that makes no demands on His followers.[5]

The Bible calls such teaching "doctrines of devils." (1 Timothy 4:1) But the Baptist pastor who had described himself as being "conservative" defended that book when we confronted him about it, and he also promoted the book in the church's newsletter.

So within the same church there was a wide variety of people. Some were faithful Christians who believed the Bible, studied it carefully, and took God seriously. Others did not really believe the Bible, and they were wide open to any strange teachings that came along. The Bible tells us not to be "...children, tossed to and fro, and carried about with every wind of doctrine, by the sleight of men, and cunning craftiness, whereby they lie in wait to deceive" (Ephesians 4:14) And it warns us:

"For the time will come when they will not endure sound doctrine; but after their own lusts shall they heap to themselves teachers, having itching ears; And they shall turn away their ears from the truth, and shall be turned unto fables." (2 Timothy 4:3-4)

We are living in times when "unthinkable" things are happening in the world and in the church. Some men who call themselves Christian pastors are actually atheists. There are so many of them that they have an online support group that helps them "move beyond faith." [6]

If Christian churches can have such a wide variety of teachings, then why couldn't satanists also have a wide variety of teachings?

In addition, a "liberal" or "moderate" satanist group could be used as a recruiting ground for identifying people who have the potential to become more hard core. Such people could be invited to participated in things that are "deeper" (i.e., more overtly evil). They would become part of an inner circle that the uninitiated were not aware of.

This could be an incremental process, bringing them into deeper and deeper depravity, but doing it one small step at a time, so that the people don't recognize the degree of change that is occurring. Incrementalism has proven to be very effective at gradually turning people into communists. (Saul Alinsky has a book titled *Rules for Radicals* which gives practical strategies for doing that.) Well, the same principles can be used to incrementally change people in other ways.

As a result, somebody could start out with satanism because it seems to be hip and cool, and his favorite musician or Hollywood actor does it. And then he could wind up taking the devil more and more seriously, and participating in rituals that are more and more overtly evil. And eventually he could get to the point that he does things like raping and murdering children in order to get spiritual power.

The starting point for such things can be something as simple as watching the Grammy Awards. In 2014 they featured a music video called "Dark Horse" that is overtly occult, and has been described by some people as being "satanic." An enthusiastic review of this music video by a popular gossip columnist referred to the two singers as being "fiery satanists." Millions of people world-wide watched the Grammy Awards, including multitudes of impressionable children. In addition, as of mid-June 2014, the online music video of "Dark Horse" had been viewed over 400 million times.[7]

Another starting point could be the Fox network TV series "Lucifer" which is scheduled to begin in 2016. The lead actor is a charming, witty man with a British accent. The devil has supposedly retired from hell and is now running a night club in Los Angeles, calling himself Lucifer Morningstar. He has red eyes, but other than that, he appears to be a handsome man who relates well to people and does good things for them. In addition, women are very attracted to him.[8]

This isn't going to be on MTV; it's being done by the Fox network. And it will be shown on prime time, when it will be seen by impressionable children. This show is being treated as if it is normal and socially acceptable. That makes it a big step towards mainstreaming satanism and enabling it to become far more popular. I would not be surprised if it results in a new genre of literature—romance novels where women fall in love with the devil.

The TV series turned out to be quite popular. So much so that it had a second series in the same year, beginning on September 19, 2016. [9]

On July 14, 2016, a hooded, robed satanist gave the opening prayer at the City Council meeting in Phoenix, Arizona.[10] The satanists were able to accomplish this by taking the City Council to Court.[11]

What Can We Do?

In the face of such evil, we need to keep reminding ourselves that God is still on His throne. The devil is on a leash. God sets limits to what the bad guys can do. Also, God's strength is made perfect in our weakness. (2 Corinthians 12:9) In addition, as Corrie ten Boom said, "If God sends us on stony paths, He provides strong shoes."

If we love God, then no matter what happens, God will use it for our long-term, eternal good. (Romans 8:28) He will use it to bring us closer to Himself, and to teach us to trust Him more, and to develop more Godly character.

That also applies to the people we love. If they love God, then God will make everything work out for their good. But if they don't love God, then nothing will do them any good. What is the use of having a pleasant life here and then going to hell?

Therefore, nobody is at the mercy of men or of circumstances. The bottom line is our relationship with God.

Do we love Him?

Chapter 8

Bathroom Battles and College Chaos

On Friday, May 13, 2016, we saw a mind-bending example of legal skill combined with a lack of wisdom, understanding, and basic common sense. The U.S. Department of Justice and the U.S. Department of Education issued their "Dear Colleague Letter on Transgender Students" which requires all public schools in the United States to allow boys into girls' restrooms and locker rooms (where girls change clothes and take showers) if they say that they "identify" as being girls.[1] This was accompanied by a press release.[2]

Supposedly, this change in gender identity can be temporary, because one of the many categories of gender is called "gender-fluid." In their article explaining what this means, CNN says that how a person "identifies" can change every day, or even every few hours.[3] As a result of this definition, a boy could call himself a boy all day long, but conveniently claim to "identify" as a girl during gym class. According to the "Dear Colleague" letter, the schools would be required to take his word for it, thus enabling that boy to watch the girls change clothes and take showers.

New York City responded to the "Dear Colleague" letter by publishing a list of 31 different genders for people to choose from.[4] In contrast, 11 states responded by filing lawsuits against the Obama administration in order to try to protect the privacy and safety of their students. They say that the government has "conspired to turn workplaces and educational settings across the country into laboratories for a massive social experiment." [5]

Some attorneys who have studied the "Dear Colleague" letter say that it can be interpreted to require colleges to allow biological males and females to spent the night together in the same hotel room on field trips, if one of them claims to identify as the other gender. Colleges are required to allow men who claim to be transgender to be roommates with one or more women. And colleges are forbidden to tell those young women or their families that their new roommate will be a man; to do so would mean risking a federal lawsuit.[6]

The Williams Institute is a public policy research institute and lobby group based at the UCLA School of Law. It was created to promote the LGBT agenda. One of their scholars wrote an article saying that 3.5% of American adults identify as being lesbian, homosexual, or bisexual, and 0.3% of adults identify as being transgender.[7] So even these LGBT activists admit that less than one-third of one percent of adults identify as being transgender, and the entire LGBT community is less than four percent of the population.

How can such a small group have such a huge impact on our culture? What are their goals? And how is this going to impact Christians?

Goal of the Sexual Anarchists

Peter LaBarbera wrote an article titled "'Gay' Power vs. Religious Liberty." In it he quotes a Canadian lawyer named Barbara Finlay who is a lesbian. She said:

> "The legal struggle for queer rights will one day be a struggle between freedom of religion versus sexual orientation."[8]

David. Kupelian's book *The Snapping of the American Mind* has many valuable insights into the times in which we are living. It includes a chapter titled "Gender Madness" which discusses the LGBT agenda. You can read that entire chapter online.[9]

Near the end of that chapter, Mr. Kupelian says that although many people thought that same-sex marriage would be the crowning achievement of the LGT movement, it has suddenly shifted its focus to "transgender rights," with *Time* magazine calling it "America's next civil rights frontier" and Vice President Joe Biden calling it "the civil rights issue of our time." Things have gotten to the point where three-year old children have been required to sign a contract promising that they won't use "transphobic language" in nursery school. Mr. Kupelian says:

> "The secret of this never-ending, always-expanding revolutionary movement, in case you haven't realized, is that it has the full support of the Far Left. Not because the Left loves homosexuals, bisexuals, and transsexuals for themselves, but because finally the Left has found its spear tip, with which—as it has dreamed of doing for decades—it can effectively attack, wound, marginalize, demonize, and criminalize its greatest enemy: the Christian religion.
>
> "Indeed, the LGBT sexual anarchy movement has the unique potential to permanently corrupt our civilization's core institution, *marriage and family*, as well as our core 'operating system,' *Judeo-Christian values*." [10]

Peter Sprigg is the Senior Fellow for Policy Studies at the Family Research Council. According to him, many LGBT activists want to destroy "the concept of gender or the separation of the genders altogether." [11] Following is an example of this approach.

Riki Wilchins is a far-left social change activist who has gone through "sex change" surgery. On April 29, he published an article about the "bathroom battles" in the homosexual publication *The Advocate*. His article is titled, "We'll Win the Bathroom Battle When the Binary Burns." What does he mean by "binary"? He describes that as being the "dominant, hetero-binary structure of boy vs. girl." [12]

I know that this kind of thinking can make your head spin, but you did read that correctly. There are some people out there who literally want to get us to the point where we become unwilling and unable to think in terms of male versus female. They don't want us to be able to tell the difference between boys and girls. And they want to train children to think like that at early ages.

Re-Defining Mental Illness

The American Psychiatric Association has officially said that being transgender is no longer considered to be a mental illness. "Gender identity disorder" has been removed from their *Diagnostic and Statistical Manual of Mental Disorders*. At this point, the condition is considered to be normal. In place of "gender identity disorder," the DSM now lists "gender dysphoria," which is emotional stress that is related to a person's gender identity. So in their eyes, the patient needs to be relieved of emotional stress, but the question of gender identity is no longer considered to be a problem.[13] Of course the next step will be to have transgender become a protected "sexual orientation."

There are some psychologists who say that "minor-attracted persons" (i.e., pedophiles) are normal. In 2003, a group of health care professionals formed an organization called B4U-Act whose purpose is to normalize pedophilia and redefine it as being a protected "sexual orientation." They are using the same tactics that were used to normalize homosexuality, which until recently was considered to be a form of mental illness.[14]

People who practice bestiality (sex with animals) also want to get on the LGBT bandwagon. An article about this is titled "Those Who Practice Bestiality Say They're Part of the Next Sexual Rights Movement."[15] One of their tactics is to come up with a nicer sounding name. They now call themselves "zoophiles" and they call bestiality "zoophilia." This can cause confusion, because "zoophile" can also mean "a person who is devoted to animals and their protection."

Politically Correct Brainwashing

Confusion is actively promoted in our public schools, where children are taught that there is no such thing as objective truth, or objective right and wrong. In law, not knowing the difference between right and wrong is called "criminal insanity." So our schools are literally teaching our children to become criminally insane. In addition, Christian faith and morals have been undermined by "values clarification" and other techniques.[16] Thomas Sowell said:

> "The techniques of brainwashing developed in totalitarian countries are routinely used in psychological conditioning programs imposed on American school children."[17]

This results in radically changing the beliefs and moral values of the children. The brainwashing techniques used on our children result in the "acceptance of alternative values by psychological rather than rational means."[18]

This brainwashing doesn't stop when the kids go to college. On the contrary, there are speech codes and Thought Police that continue this process of undermining faith, morals, and rational thinking. This can result in having some young people literally become sociopaths.

This doesn't stop when people leave college. The state of California is "poised to make it illegal to question global warming." They are trying to make it a crime to have scientific opinions that are not politically correct.[19]

An American college professor is demanding that people who deny "climate change" be sent to prison for being "criminally negligent."[20] U.S. Senator Whitehouse also wants to see "climate change deniers" be sent to prison.[21]

By now, some readers are probably saying, "But nobody would do *that*!" I know the feeling well. I often had to deal with it myself while doing the research for this book. The answer is that decent people wouldn't do it, but some people would. And they have managed to get themselves into positions of power and authority and influence.

Means, Motive, and Opportunity

In criminal law, the judge looks to see if the alleged perpetrator had the "means, motive, and opportunity." Well, mandatory public schooling provides the opportunity. So does the entertainment business—using TV, movies, video games, music videos, Superbowl half-time shows, rock concerts, etc.

The manipulative aspects of behavioral psychology provide the means. This can be taught to non-psychologists who don't understand what they are really doing. One example of that is teachers. But what is the motive?

When it comes to the LGBT community, some of their motive is the desire to engage in "free sex" to a degree that some have described as being "sexual anarchy." But there is more to it than that, because people have done such things for years without trying to force the rest of the world to actively endorse what they are doing, much less trying to indoctrinate young children to accept such things.

Two motives are humanism, and communism. Both have been increasing exponentially in our society in recent years. As we will see later, humanism is being promoted in our public schools.

For an example of how communism has been gaining in power, we only need to look at our current President. When he was young, Obama was mentored by Frank Marshall Davis, who was a prominent communist activist.[22] When he was a community organizer in Chicago, Obama was mentored by Saul Alinsky, who is a well-known communist activist. After he was elected President, Saul's son L. David Alinsky published an article in the *Boston Globe* praising Obama's training by Saul Alinsky. He said:

> "Barack Obama's training in Chicago by the great community organizers is showing its effectiveness... [I]t is a powerful strategy for initiating change and making it really happen. Obama learned his lesson well." [23]

Occultism and communism can overlap. People usually think of communists as being atheists. However, Karl Marx was actually a satanist. Pastor Richard Wurmbrand makes a persuasive case for that in his book *Was Karl Marx a Satanist?* We can also see the communist-satanist connection from the fact that the notorious American communist Saul Alinsky dedicated his book *Rules for Radicals* to Lucifer, who he called "the very first radical." [24]

Goals of Communism and Humanism

With communism, you need to look at their goals. On January 10, 1963, a congressman read 45 communist goals into the *Congressional Record*. You can read them online.[25] These were excerpted from Cleon Skousen's book *The Naked Communist*. They include the following:

- Undermine cultural standards of morality
- Make sexual anarchy appear to be "normal, natural, healthy"
- Infiltrate churches and undermine belief in the Bible
- Take control of the psychiatric profession and use it to get coercive control over people
- Discredit and undermine the family
- Reduce parental influence over children

What about humanism? It is openly hostile to Christianity and traditional family values. Its antagonism can be seen in the following quotation from the British Humanist Association:

"Some opponents of Humanism have accused us of wishing to overthrow the traditional Christian family. They are right. That is exactly what we intend to do." [26]

This kind of attitude is destructive for society. And the people who promote it will pay a price for doing that. The Bible says,

"Woe unto them that call evil good, and good evil; that put darkness for light, and light for darkness; that put bitter for sweet, and sweet for bitter!" (Isaiah 5:20)

Biblical Encouragement And Guidance

*"Trust in the Lord with all thine heart;
and lean not unto thine own understanding.
In all thy ways acknowledge him,
and he shall direct thy paths."*
(Proverbs 3:5-6)

Chapter 9

Dealing With Shock

"Yea, and all that will live godly in Christ Jesus shall suffer persecution." (2 Timothy 3:12)

Persecution is shocking. It's cruel and unfair. Why do people punish us for doing good? Why do they hate us for loving Jesus? I just doesn't make sense. It seems crazy.

It certainly doesn't make sense to reasonable people who know God and have a Biblical standard of right and wrong. In contrast, the devil's values are upside down, and he is literally insane. He had to be, in order to think that he could fight against God and win.

As Christians serve God, they increasingly see things from His perspective. Those who serve the devil (whether knowingly or unknowingly) wind up thinking more and more the way that he does.

Many people blame God when cruel and unjust things are done to them. But they are accusing the wrong person. They should be blaming Adam and Eve instead of God. Everything bad that happens to us is because Adam and Eve rebelled against God in the Garden of Eden.

Try to put yourself in God's shoes for a moment. He created a perfect world in which everything was good. Adam and Eve were created as mature adults, ready for marriage. They never had a troubled childhood. They didn't have any old wounds or scars. They had a closeness to God that we can't begin to comprehend, walking and talking with Him every evening. Their world was beautiful and safe. They were healthy and had wonderful things to eat all around them, waiting to be picked and enjoyed. All of their needs were met, and all of their desires were fulfilled.

Then along came the serpent, who was the world's first con artist. He talked them into rebelling against God.

When everything was perfect, both Adam and Eve fell into sin. That is a 100 percent rate of failure. Now, if having everything be perfect doesn't work, then what is the only alternative? Suffering. Hardship. Death. Discovering that we desperately need God.

My Mom wrote a poem about the shock and challenge of having normal life suddenly be radically changed in painful and confusing ways:

TRUST
(by Frances Morrisson) (My Mom)

*Suddenly the Everyday
is wrenched away.*

*Lord, please guard and grow
the fullness of my love and trust in You.*

*When all I know
is set afloat today,
pilot my boat and nudge me to
the harbor of the Narrow Way*

*There let me find a clearer, newer view
where all that's upside down
resolves; makes sense;
steady in the light of love and Trust in You.*

"Wrenched away" is a good description of what persecution feels like. This applies to a Christian baker who has been threatened with prison because he refused to bake a wedding cake for a homosexual marriage,[1] and it also applies to a Christian in the Middle East who is beheaded because of his faith. It's shocking, and something inside us cries out, "This can't be happening!" There is distress and grief, pain and confusion.

Obviously, what the baker suffered is not as serious as being beheaded, but it's still a shock. There is a difference in the degree of severity of the persecution, but it's a gut-wrenching event for the people involved in both situations. Comparing it to animals, it is better to be attacked by an angry bobcat than by a man-eating tiger. However, either way, there is a lot of suffering involved.

The best antidote for shock and pain and suffering is the Word of God. It is also the best guide for how to respond to the challenges of life. Therefore, I'm going to quote a lot of Scripture.

The Bible tells us that Christians should expect to be persecuted. However, until recently, American Christians were usually treated well. This feels normal for us, but it is unusual in terms of the world, since many countries have serious persecution. Now Christians in the United States are suffering for their faith. For Americans, this is shocking, but according to the Bible, we should not be surprised:

> "And he said to them all, If any man will come after me, let him deny himself, and take up his cross daily, and follow me." (Luke 9:23)

> "Yea, and all that will live godly in Christ Jesus shall suffer persecution." (2 Timothy 3:12)

> "Remember the word that I said unto you. The servant is not greater than his lord. If they have persecuted me, they will also persecute you; if they have kept my saying, they will keep yours also." (John 15:20)

> "We are troubled on every side, yet not distressed; we are perplexed, but not in despair; Persecuted, but not forsaken; cast down, but not destroyed" (2 Corinthians 4:8-9)

"Who shall separate us from the love of Christ? Shall tribulation, or distress, or persecution, or famine, or nakedness, or peril, or sword? As it is written, For thy sake we are killed all the day long; we are accounted as sheep for the slaughter. Nay, in all these things we are more than conquerors through him that loved us." (Romans 8:35-37)

The good news is that God enables His people to endure persecution. His grace is sufficient to get us through the trials and tribulations, and if we love Him, then He will make whatever we go through work out for our good:

"I can do all things through Christ which strengtheneth me." (Philippians 4:13)

"And he said unto me, My grace is sufficient for thee: for my strength is made perfect in weakness. Most gladly therefore will I rather glory in my infirmities, that the power of Christ may rest upon me." (2 Corinthians 12:9)

"These things I have spoken unto you, that in me ye might have peace. In the world ye shall have tribulation: but be of good cheer; I have overcome the world." (John 16:33)

"And we know that all things work together for good to them that love God, to them who are the called according to his purpose." (Romans 8:28)

According to the Bible, God uses trials and tribulations to build Godly character in us. This is good fruit in our lives, and it will be a blessing for us and for others. The suffering is temporary, but the rewards will be eternal:

"Beloved, think it not strange concerning the fiery trial which is to try you, as though some strange thing happened unto you: But rejoice, inasmuch as ye are partakers of Christ's sufferings; that, when his glory shall be revealed, ye may be glad also with exceeding joy. If ye be reproached for the name of Christ, happy are ye; for the spirit of glory and of God resteth upon you: on their part he is evil spoken of, but on your part he is glorified" (1 Peter 4:12-14)

"My brethren, count it all joy when ye fall into divers temptations; Knowing this, that the trying of your faith worketh patience. But let patience have her perfect work, that ye may be perfect and entire, wanting nothing." (James 1:2-4)

"…we glory in tribulations also: knowing that tribulation worketh patience; And patience, experience; and experience, hope: And hope maketh not ashamed; because the love of God is shed abroad in our hearts by the Holy Ghost which is given unto us." (Romans 5:3-5)

Jesus told us that it is a blessing to be persecuted for His sake. Now in terms of my emotions, I have real difficulty with that. I want to avoid suffering, and it pains me to see others suffer. However, God sees the big picture. I don't. God knows what He is talking about.

My perspective is limited by my natural fears. Therefore, I need to take God at His word and believe Him, in spite of the fact that what He says goes against the grain. Here is what Jesus said:

"Blessed are they which are persecuted for righteousness' sake: for theirs is the kingdom of heaven." (Matthew 5:10)

"Blessed are ye, when men shall revile you, and persecute you, and shall say all manner of evil against you falsely, for my sake. Rejoice, and be exceeding glad: for great is your reward in heaven: for so persecuted they the prophets which were before you." (Matthew 5:11-12)

I am not at the point of being able to "rejoice" or be "exceeding glad" if I am persecuted, or if people I know and love are persecuted. However, I can tell God, "This does not feel like a blessing to me, but You say that it is a blessing. Please change my heart, and enable me to see it the way that You see it."

There is a story about a little boy who was with his father during a terrorist attack. There was gunfire, and shouting, and confusion. When it was all over, the father asked his son, "Were you afraid?" And his boy answered, "No, Daddy. You were holding my hand."

That's the way that we need to be with the Lord.

God is faithful. He loves us. He promised that He will always be with us. And He knows what He is doing. He sees the really big picture. We can't comprehend it yet.

GOD'S LOVE
(by Maria Kneas)

The God who made the earth has always loved us.
Before we drew a breath, our heart was known.
God created us to live with Him forever,
To sing and dance with joy before His throne.

Our time on earth is hard, but it is fleeting.
No matter how things seem, God's always there.
He'll guide us and protect us and watch over us,
And take away each tear and fear and care.

And when the toil and pain and fear have ended,
When sorrow's gone, and all we know is love,
Then we and God will celebrate forever,
Rejoicing with the saints in Heaven above.

Chapter 10

Fighting Fear

"And the Lord, he it is that doth go before thee; he will be with thee, he will not fail thee, neither forsake thee: fear not, neither be dismayed." (Deuteronomy 31:8)

I know something about fighting fear because I've had a problem with fear all of my life. My Dad was sent home from World War II in a hospital ship after attempting suicide, and my Mom was always afraid that he would try it again.

Fear is contagious. Children pick up what their parents are feeling. Every night, I had a nightmare about being chased by something that was horrible, but I didn't know what it was.

When I was 15 years old, Mom told me to let Dad know that dinner was ready. I found him lying in bed, unconscious from an attempt to commit suicide. Mercifully, we discovered him soon enough, and he recovered at the hospital.

I married a strong, healthy young man, and three years into our marriage, he had a massive heart attack. He needed a quadruple bypass, but wasn't strong enough to get the surgery because of the damage done to his heart. After a year of living with painful and debilitating heart problems, he died. During that year, every day when I was at work, I never knew if I would find him dead on the floor when I came home.

There have been other fearful things in my life, including cancer. The point is, even without persecution, we have to deal with fear. Drastic things can happen suddenly, without warning.

I had to overcome some fear in order to write this book, because the people who hate Christianity will not appreciate having this book be published. Some of those people work in our government. According to official government documents, I am an "extremist" and a "potential terrorist" because I am an Evangelical Christian, I take what the Bible says about the End Times seriously, and I believe that unborn babies should not be killed.[1]

Love is an antidote to fear. Therefore, anything that we can do to increase our love for God and for one another will help get rid of fear. The Bible says:

> "There is no fear in love; but perfect love casteth out fear: because fear hath torment. He that feareth is not made perfect in love." (1 John 4:18)

Our natural human love is inadequate. However, we can ask God to give us His love, to enable us to love the way that He does. The Bible says that He can do that:

> "And hope maketh not ashamed; because **the love of God is shed abroad in our hearts by the Holy Ghost** which is given unto us." (Romans 5:5, emphasis added)

God can enable us to do things that we would never be able to do in our own strength. We are weak, but He is strong. And He is faithful to help His own. The Bible says:

> "I can do all things through Christ which strengtheneth me." (Philippians 4:13)

> "The Lord is my light and my salvation; whom shall I fear? the Lord is the strength of my life; of whom shall I be afraid?" (Psalm 27:1)

> "My flesh and my heart faileth: but God is the strength of my heart, and my portion for ever." (Psalm 73:26)

> "Who shall separate us from the love of Christ? shall tribulation, or distress, or persecution, or famine, or nakedness, or peril, or sword? As it is written, For thy sake we are killed all the day long; we are accounted as sheep for the slaughter. Nay, in all these things we are more than conquerors through him that loved us." (Romans 8:35-37)

> "And he said unto me, My grace is sufficient for thee: for my strength is made perfect in weakness. Most gladly therefore will I rather glory in my infirmities, that the power of Christ may rest upon me." (2 Corinthians 12:9)

> "These things I have spoken unto you, that in me ye might have peace. In the world ye shall have tribulation: but be of good cheer; I have overcome the world." (John 16:33)

A good antidote to the fear of what men can do to us is the "fear of the Lord." This involves more than just reverence. It also includes the fear of God's punishment. If our love isn't strong enough to enable us to do what is right, then the fear of the Lord can give us the strength to do it. Jesus said:

> "And fear not them which kill the body, but are not able to kill the soul: but rather fear him which is able to destroy both soul and body in hell." (Matthew 10:28)

According to the Bible, the fear of the Lord also gives us wisdom and understanding. It enables us to be rightly related to God.

It's good when we can do the right thing because we love God. But when we are unable to do that, then we can recognize God's power and authority, salute Him, and say, "Yes, Sir!"

My Dad used to talk about the importance of "taking God seriously." That includes the fear of the Lord. The Bible talks about how important it is:

> "The fear of the Lord is the beginning of wisdom: and the knowledge of the holy is understanding." (Proverbs 9:10)

> "Behold, the eye of the Lord is upon them that fear him, upon them that hope in his mercy" (Psalm 33:18)

> "The angel of the Lord encampeth round about them that fear him, and delivereth them." (Psalm 34:7)

There is a song based on that last Scripture about the angel of the Lord protecting those who fear Him. One night I had to walk through a dangerous neighborhood, and I was afraid. As I walked, I quietly sang that song. I started out feeling afraid, but as I kept singing, the fear decreased. And God protected me.

Another antidote to fear is keeping the big picture in mind—eternity. This world is not really our home. We are citizens of the Kingdom of God. Our true home is Heaven, and our true king is Almighty God.

The Apostle Paul said that we are "ambassadors" for Jesus Christ:

> "Now then we are ambassadors for Christ" (2 Corinthians 5:20)

Think about what it means to be an ambassador. You have to leave your native land and live in another country, surrounded by people whose customs and values are different from yours. They may even be cruel and barbaric. (Can you imagine what it would be like to be an ambassador in a place like North Korea or Saudi Arabia?) You are only there temporarily, representing the government of your own country. At some point, your ruler will call you back to your native land.

The book *Pilgrim's Progress* describes us as being pilgrims on a journey through this world, on our way to Heaven. An old spiritual has the same theme. Sometimes I sing this song when I read distressing news about what is going on in the world:

POOR WAYFARING STRANGER
(19th century, public domain)

I am a poor wayfaring stranger
Traveling through this world of woe
But there's no trouble, toil or danger
In that bright land to which I go.

It helps to remember that our time here on earth is only temporary, and that this world is passing away. Here are two Scripture passages that give us the eternal perspective. I often think about this. The one from the Book of Revelation is one of my favorite passages in the Bible:

> "Nevertheless we, according to his promise, look for new heavens and a new earth, wherein dwelleth righteousness." (2 Peter 3:13)

> "And God shall wipe away all tears from their eyes; and there shall be no more death, neither sorrow, nor crying, neither shall there be any more pain: for the former things are passed away. And he that sat upon the throne said, Behold, I make all things new." (Revelation 21:4-5)

Sometimes worship can dispel fear. About 20 years ago, a mammogram showed signs of possible cancer in both of my breasts, and I had to get a biopsy done. I asked my surgeon to use a local anesthesia, because that is less stressful to the body, and he agreed to do so. I wound up with two doctors cutting on me at the same time (one working on each breast). Evidently they forgot that I was awake, because they were talking about seeing things that looked like cancer.

That was a frightening situation. The more they talked, the greater my fear became. Then I remembered a Scripture passage:

> "I will bless the Lord at all times: his praise shall continually be in my mouth." (Psalm 34:1)

They were playing music in the operating room. I asked them to turn it off, which they did. Then I began to sing a worship song based on Scripture. By the time I finished singing the first line of that song, the fear just drained away.

All during that procedure, I kept on singing. One of the nurses knew the songs, and she sang along with me. I was at peace, focussed on God instead of my ailing body. I was thinking about God's love and faithfulness, instead of worrying about my future.

(I had a double radical mastectomy, followed by chemotherapy. The hardships I went through brought me closer to God. Being faced with your mortality changes your priorities, and it makes you know that you **need** God.)

No matter what happens to us, God is always worthy of our praise. The Bible says:

> "O magnify the Lord with me, and let us exalt his name together." (Psalm 34:3)

When we "magnify" the Lord, we don't make Him bigger. He is already much greater than we can possibly comprehend. What we do is make ourselves more capable of recognizing His greatness. When we do that, God seems larger to us, which makes our problems seem smaller by comparison. Here are some Scriptures that remind us of how great and mighty our God is:

"Thus saith the Lord, The heaven is my throne, and the earth is my footstool" (Isaiah 66:1)

"When I consider thy heavens, the work of thy fingers, the moon and the stars, which thou hast ordained" (Psalm 8:3)

"I am God, and there is none else; I am God, and there is none like me, Declaring the end from the beginning, and from ancient times the things that are not yet done, saying, My counsel shall stand, and I will do all my pleasure" (Isaiah 46:9-10)

"The heavens declare the glory of God; and the firmament sheweth his handywork." (Psalm 19:1)

One thing that can cause fear is sins that we have not dealt with. That puts a barrier between us and God, which makes it more difficult for us to turn to Him and to trust Him. Therefore, it is good to habitually invite God to search our hearts and show us if there is anything that we need to repent of. King David said:

"Who can understand his errors? cleanse thou me from secret faults. Keep back thy servant also from presumptuous sins; let them not have dominion over me: then shall I be upright, and I shall be innocent from the great transgression. Let the words of my mouth, and the meditation of my heart, be acceptable in thy sight, O Lord, my strength, and my redeemer." (Psalm 19:12-14)

"Search me, O God, and know my heart: try me, and know my thoughts: And see if there be any wicked way in me, and lead me in the way everlasting." (Psalm 139:23-24)

"Create in me a clean heart, O God; and renew a right spirit within me." (Psalm 51:10)

America has become a sex-saturated society. As a result, much of our entertainment contains things that are intended to incite lust. So do many commercials. Jesus warned us:

"But I say unto you, That whosoever looketh on a woman to lust after her hath committed adultery with her already in his heart." (Matthew 5:28)

Obviously, that principle applies to women as well as to men. Our society takes such things lightly, but God takes them very seriously:

"Now the works of the flesh are manifest, which are these; **Adultery**, **fornication**, uncleanness, **lasciviousness** [lustful], Idolatry, witchcraft, hatred, variance [contentions], emulations [jealousy], wrath, strife, seditions, heresies, Envyings, murders, drunkenness, revellings, and such like: of the which I tell you before, as I have also told you in time past, that **they which do such things shall not inherit the kingdom of God**." (Galatians 5:19-21, emphasis added)

Obviously, nobody is going to be perfect this side of Heaven. We will keep falling into sin. The point is, when we sin, are we distressed about it? Do we repent? Do we make a serious effort to stop doing it? Do we keep asking God to help us overcome it? Are we doing it more and more, and getting hardened to it? Or are we doing it less and less? What direction are we moving in?

When it comes to repenting for sins, abortion can be a real stumbling block, because the world keeps telling us that what a pregnant woman has inside her is not a baby. The problem is, how can you repent for something that you think is not a sin?

This is a strange double standard, because the world will put Americans in jail for destroying an eagle's egg. They know that there is a baby eagle in there. Everybody knows that a pregnant cat has kittens inside her, and a pregnant dog has puppies inside her.

(Before I go any further about this subject, I want to remind anybody who has had an abortion that God will forgive you if you repent. He loves you.)

The world tells us that what a pregnant woman has inside her is only a "fetus." Well, the word "fetus" is just a Latin word that means "child." Doctors like using Latin terms for things.

There are photos of babies in the womb who are sucking their thumbs. They are obviously babies. Even sonograms can be clear enough to show that.

The Bible makes it obvious that what a woman carries inside her is a baby. In the Gospel of Luke, we are told that Mary became pregnant supernaturally when the Holy Spirit came upon her. Then she went to visit her cousin Elizabeth, who was six months pregnant with John the Baptist.

As soon as Mary walked into the room, carrying her recently conceived baby in her womb, the baby inside Elizabeth's womb recognized Jesus and leaped for joy. We are also told that John the Baptist was filled with the Holy Spirit while he was still inside his mother's womb:

> "And it came to pass, that, when Elisabeth heard the salutation of Mary, the babe leaped in her womb; and **Elisabeth was filled with the Holy Ghost**: And she spake out with a loud voice, and said, Blessed art thou among women, and blessed is the fruit of thy womb. And whence is this to me, that the mother of my Lord should come to me? For, lo, **as soon as the voice of thy salutation sounded in mine ears, the babe leaped in my womb for joy**." (Luke 1:41-44, emphasis added)

"For he shall be great in the sight of the Lord, and shall drink neither wine nor strong drink; and **he shall be filled with the Holy Ghost, even from his mother's womb.**" (Luke 1:15, emphasis added)

God can call a person to ministry before they are born. We see this with the prophet Jeremiah. God told him:

"Before I formed thee in the belly I knew thee; and before thou camest forth out of the womb I sanctified thee, and I ordained thee a prophet unto the nations." (Jeremiah 1:5)

If you have had an abortion, or have encouraged anybody else to have one, then please repent. God will forgive you. He loves you.

You might find it helpful to read Psalm 51. David wrote it after the prophet Nathan confronted him about committing adultery with Bathsheba and setting up her husband Uriah to be killed, which was a way of murdering him. David repented, and the Bible says that David had a heart for God. (1 Kings 11:4) In the Gospels, Jesus is called the "son of David." (Matthew 9:27, 15:22; Mark 10:47-48)

One thing that can cause fear is the fact that occultism is becoming mainstream. There are satanists and witches who put spells and curses on Christians. In case you think that such things are not real, the Bible says that they are:

"And Moses and Aaron went in unto Pharaoh, and they did so as the Lord had commanded: and Aaron cast down his rod before Pharaoh, and before his servants, and it became a serpent. Then Pharaoh also called the wise men and the sorcerers: now the magicians of Egypt, they also did in like manner with their enchantments. For they cast down every man his rod, and they became serpents: but Aaron's rod swallowed up their rods." (Exodus 7:10-12)

Notice that Aaron did something supernatural in the power of God, and then Pharoah's sorcerers did the same kind of thing, using "enchantments" (spells). However, Pharoah's sorcerers were not able to harm Moses or Aaron, because Aaron's serpent ate ("swallowed") the serpents of the sorcerers.

The bad news is that occult power is very real. The good news is that God is infinitely greater, and He takes care of His own. He is willing and able to protect us.

When you drive down a country road, you can go off that road on either side and wind up in a ditch. When it comes to the occult, there are two ditches that we can fall into.

One ditch is to deny the existence and power of the devil and his demons. This means denying the Bible, because Jesus is often shown casting out demons. And according to Mark 16:17, Jesus gave those who believe in Him the power to cast out demons. We see a number of examples of this in the Book of Acts.

The other ditch is to "see a demon behind every bush," as the saying goes. Here's an example from my life. I'm overweight. One day I was eating a candy bar, and a woman who claimed to have a deliverance ministry tried to cast a "demon of chocolate" out of me. That kind of nonsense gives Christians a bad name.

When God confronts the devil, it is **not** like a wrestling match. It is more like squashing a bug with your finger, or flicking a fly off your shoulder. Almighty God has absolute power over the devil. God allows him to do some things, but the devil is on a leash, and eventually he will be thrown into the Lake of Fire. (Revelation 20:10) Look at what Jesus said:

> "But if I **with the finger of God cast out devils**, no doubt the kingdom of God is come upon you." (Luke 11:20, emphasis added)

> "Behold, I give unto you power to tread on serpents and scorpions, and **over all the power of the enemy**: and

nothing shall by any means hurt you." (Luke 10:19, emphasis added)

We see a physical example of this when the Apostle Paul was bitten by a poisonous snake. The natives knew that this snake was deadly, and they expected Paul to die, but it didn't harm him at all:

"And when Paul had gathered a bundle of sticks, and laid them on the fire, **there came a viper out of the heat, and fastened on his hand**. And when the barbarians saw the venomous beast hang on his hand, they said among themselves, No doubt this man is a murderer, whom, though he hath escaped the sea, yet vengeance suffereth not to live. And he shook off the beast into the fire, and **felt no harm**. Howbeit they looked when he should have swollen, or fallen down dead suddenly: but after they had looked a great while, and **saw no harm come to him**, they changed their minds, and said that he was a god." (Acts 28:3-6, emphasis added)

What happened to Paul demonstrates God's protection from deadly physical things. However, the "power of the enemy" means spiritual dangers as well as physical ones. God is able to protect us from curses and spells.

God protects us. However, the Bible also tells us that we should protect ourselves by putting on the "armor of God." We are to be active, not passive:

"Finally, my brethren, be strong in the Lord, and in the power of his might. Put on the whole armour of God, that ye may be able to stand against the wiles of the devil. For we wrestle not against flesh and blood, but against principalities, against powers, against the rulers of the darkness of this world, against spiritual wickedness in high places. Wherefore take unto you the whole armour of God, that ye may be able to withstand in the evil day, and having done all, to stand. Stand therefore, having your loins girt about with **truth**, and having on the breastplate of **righteousness**; And your feet shod with the preparation of the gospel of peace; Above all, taking the shield of **faith**, wherewith ye shall be able to quench all the fiery darts of the wicked. And take the helmet of salvation, and the sword of the Spirit, which is the **word of God**: **Praying always** with all prayer and supplication in the Spirit, and watching thereunto with all perseverance and supplication for all saints" (Ephesians 6:10-18, emphasis added)

According to this passage, we are not to be passive. God expects us to love the truth, have faith, get the Word of God in us (develop a working knowlege of the Bible by reading it and studying it), and pray "always." Obviously, we can't be on our knees praying all day long, but we can have a spirit of prayer. We can be aware of God, and stay in communication with Him throughout the day.

Before my husband died, we could be in the same room, doing different things, and not talking to one another. However, we felt one another's presence. We were aware of the other person, even when we were intensely focussed on something else. There was an awareness of the one we love, and it was easy to talk from time to time.

We can be the same way with God. We can have times of intense prayer, but we can also talk with Him as we go about our daily routines—when we are cooking, or walking somewhere, or driving, or eating a meal.

God has ways of communicating with us. One of them is bringing Scriptures to mind. Another is nudging us, like a sheep dog nudges the sheep to get them to go where they need to be:

"But the Comforter, which is the Holy Ghost, whom the Father will send in my name, he shall teach you all things, and bring all things to your remembrance, whatsoever I have said unto you." (John 14:26)

"My sheep hear my voice, and I know them, and they follow me" (John 10:27)

A good example of God leading us (or nudging us) is the Christian mother whose son is a soldier in Afghanistan. One night she wakes up, feeling an urgent need to pray for her boy, so she prays her heart out for him. Then several weeks later, she gets a letter from her son, saying that his unit was ambushed. Some men were killed, and others were wounded, but he was not harmed. The mother looks at the date when the ambush occurred, and she realizes that it happened during the time when she was praying for her boy.

For an excellent study of the Armor of God, I recommend the website *The Shepherd's Way*. Look at the section titled "The Armor of God." (The Internet address of the website ends with "dot-**to**" rather than "dot-com.")

www.shepherd.**to**

In addition to this article, under the section titled "Bible Studies" there is a more in-depth study of this called "A Wardrobe from the King." This is a series of studies (one for each piece of the armor).

The Bible tells us to "cast" our cares (fears, anxieties, worries, and concerns) on God because He cares for us (loves us and takes good care of us). That means giving our cares to God, and leaving them with Him—not taking them back again:

"Casting all your care upon him; for he careth for you." (1 Peter 5:7)

This is easier said than done. We have to learn how to do it. Like many things in life, it takes practice. We can ask God to enable us to do it, to give us the grace for it, and to help us appropriate and work with the grace that He gives us.

This morning, a prayer came to me. I would like to share it with you. The prayer is based on some Scripture passages, so I'll give them first:

"And **let the peace of God rule in your hearts**, to the which also ye are called in one body; and be ye thankful." (Colossians 3:15, emphasis added)

"For it is God which worketh in you both **to will** and **to do** of his good pleasure." (Philippians 2:13, emphasis added)

"O Lord, thou art our father; we are the clay, and thou our potter; and we all are the work of thy hand." (Isaiah 64:8)
"There is no fear in love; but **perfect love casteth out fear**: because fear hath torment. He that feareth is not made perfect in love." (1 John 4:18, emphasis added)

"**Ye are the light of the world**. A city that is set on an hill cannot be hid." (Matthew 5:14, emphasis added)

"**Let your light so shine before men**, that they may see your good works, and glorify your Father which is in heaven." (Matthew 5:16, emphasis added)

"That ye may be blameless and harmless, the sons of God, without rebuke, in the midst of a crooked and perverse nation, among whom ye **shine as lights in the world**" (Philippians 2:15, emphasis added)

"Herein is my Father glorified, that ye bear much fruit; so shall ye be my disciples." (John 15:8)

PRAYER:

Lord, how do I let Your peace rule in my heart? You told me to do it, which means that it is possible to do it, and You expect me to do it. However, I have fear and anxiety in my heart, which means that Your peace is not ruling in me. Please forgive me for not doing what You told me to do.

Lord, I don't know how to do it. Please show me how. Teach me. Put the "willing" and the "doing" in me. You are the Creator. I'm just a creature. You are my Father. I'm just a child. You are the potter. I'm just the clay. Please change me. Show me how to do it. Make me into a person who does it as a way of life.

Lord, please give me the grace to do it, and help me cooperate with Your grace. Deal with anything in me that hinders your peace, that blocks it in any way. Be glorified in my life. Fill me with Your peace and Your love in a way that gives You glory.

You said that perfect love casts out fear. But I have fear in my heart. That means that I don't have enough love for You or for others. My love isn't good enough. It isn't strong enough. Please put Your love in my heart. Let Your love be shed abroad in my heart.

You told us to be lights in the darkness. Showing Your peace and Your love in the midst of trials and tribulations is one way of doing that.

I want to bear good fruit for Your Kingdom, and this fear and worry are getting in the way. Please set me free from them. In Jesus' name. Amen.

JESUS, SON OF DAVID
(by Maria Kneas)

Jesus, son of David, have mercy on me.

Light my path and guide my way.
Make me faithful, so I'll stay
Close to You throughout the day,
Devoted to You in every way.

Jesus, son of David, have mercy on me.

Open my eyes that I may see
The precious truth that You have for me.
Open my heart to love as You do.
Enable me to be faithful and true.

Jesus, son of David, have mercy on me.

*(In Mark 10:47-48, blind Bartimaeus cried out,
"Jesus, thou son of David, have mercy on me.")*

Chapter 11

Handling Grief

"...weeping may endure for a night, but joy cometh in the morning." (Psalm 30:5)

I've been grieving for our nation ever since Obama got elected back in 2008. As things ramp up, we will have more and more reasons to grieve. And it's not just the state of the nation. Even worse is the state of so much of what calls itself the Church.

In addition, persecution is increasing. And we could face our equivalent of a Kristallnacht some day: a game-changing event that enables the bad guys to start doing some serious persecution of real Christians, and of political dissidents. When that happens, then we will have stronger, more personal reasons for grieving than we do at present. Therefore I want to share some things that I learned when my husband Ray died.

When your heart is broken, it will never be the same again. And at that point, we have a choice to make. Are we going to allow our heart to turn in on itself and get smaller? Or will we choose to open it out more and have our heart become larger and more loving?

After Ray died, it became clear to me that I needed to make a decision to open my heart up more and become more loving towards more and more people. So looked around to see who I could show love to.

I lived in an apartment, and I noticed that people only talked to the resident manager when they had a problem or a complaint. So I made a point of stopping by to encourage her. I found an old lady in the building who needed somebody to hang pictures, and turn her mattress, and talk with her, and listen to her. I made sandwiches for the street people in our neighborhood. Eventually

I wound up being a live-in housemother for mentally retarded adults.

Something else became apparent. I became grateful that Ray had died first. Because that way, he didn't have to go through the grieving. He was spared having to go through all that. It would have been so hard on him. Therefore, it was better for Ray to go first, and leave the grieving to me.

Grief is physically and emotionally tiring. It is also distracting. We are living a normal life (or trying to), but part of us is off somewhere else dealing with that grief. As a result, our minds don't work as well. We forget things. We make mistakes in thinking.

This is a temporary thing. With time, the intensity of the heaviness will lift. And after that, our thinking will get back to normal.

Whenever I go to a funeral I always tell that to the families of the person who died. And they are always relieved to hear it. One man asked me to tell it all to them a second time. It was such a relief to find out that they weren't having a mental problem. That it was just a normal byproduct of grieving.

However, there is a difference between the kind of grief that a person would have, living in a free society, when a loved one dies, and the kind of grief that they would have living under a Gestapo who murdered their loved one. In that case, they have to forgive the murderers. And they have to deal with the constant pressure and fear created by living under a Gestapo.

No matter what anybody has done to us, or to people we love, we have to forgive them. Because if we don't, then bitterness and unforgiveness will eat us up like cancer. Forgiving isn't easy, but by the grace of God, it is possible. That's why I devoted an entire chapter to it ("Jesus Told Us to Forgive").

When it comes to being subjected to intense pressure, it helps to remember what happens to divers who do deep sea diving. The pressure down there is strong enough to crush a man to death. However, if he has a pressurized diving suit, and the pressure inside the suit matches the pressure that is outside of it, then he won't be harmed.

We Christians have the Holy Spirit dwelling inside us. Therefore, as the outside pressure increases, the inside pressure from the presence of the Holy Spirit in us can increase enough to prevent us from being crushed by that external pressure. As a result, Christians can spiritually and emotionally survive things that would destroy a nonbeliever.

One thing that is helpful is to develop the habit of thanking and praising the Lord. And to develop a "vocabulary" of worship songs. I'm struck with how often I've read about Christians who were martyred, and they died holding hands and singing hymns or worship songs together.

> "I will bless the Lord at all times: his praise shall continually be in my mouth. My soul shall make her boast in the Lord: the humble shall hear thereof, and be glad. O magnify the Lord with me, and let us exalt his name together." (Psalm 34:1-3)

One striking example of the power of God to sustain a believer is the death of the martyr John Hus. He was burned at the stake. But he never screamed. You would expect a man who was being burned alive to be screaming with pain. But instead, he was singing. He started singing to God before they set the wood on fire, and he kept right on singing until he died.

I don't know how God enabled John Hus to do that. But if God could do that for him, then He can do comparable things for us, if we ever need them.

No matter what happens to us, or to those we love, our God is willing and able to sustain us, and keep us going, for as long as He has work for us to do down here. When we get to Heaven, we will discover that God did wonderful things in our lives while we were going through those very difficult times. The pain and pressure will fade away, like mist disappears when the sun comes up. And we will rejoice with God, and with those who truly love Him, forever and ever and ever.

> "For which cause we faint not; but though our outward man perish, yet the inward man is renewed day by day. For our light affliction, which is but for a moment, worketh for us a far more exceeding and eternal weight of glory; While we look not at the things which are seen, but at the things which are not seen: for the things which are seen are temporal; but the things which are not seen are eternal." (2 Corinthians 4:16-18)

> "Blessed are they that mourn: for they shall be comforted." (Matthew 5:4)

> "And God shall wipe away all tears from their eyes; and there shall be no more death, neither sorrow, nor crying, neither shall there be any more pain: for the former things are passed away." (Revelation 21:4)

BLESSED IN THE CRUCIBLE
(by Frances Morrisson) (my Mom)

O be blessed, by our Creator:
The One who stretched out the heavens
by the breath of His mouth;
and declared out of nothingness LIGHT!
And all forms of LIFE!
the One who woos us beyond the Curse and our resistance;
the One who gives each life a glorious purpose.

O Lord:
You gave us hearts, and breath, minds and limbs
to welcome, and be nourished, by Your Love and Word;
to seek Your Wisdom, strength and Ways;
to carry Faith in Hope, to Your gates of Justice:
washed in Your Love, strengthened by Your Mercy.

O Lord:
How can we utter our praise high enough,
deep enough, with fullest joy in harmony?
How can we murmur our love beautifully enough?
How can we bask peacefully enough in Your Presence?
How can we spread Your message clearly enough?

But these we try, blessed in the crucible of living Life.

Chapter 12

The Bottom Line

"...choose you this day whom ye will serve... but as for me and my house, we will serve the LORD." (Joshua 24:15)

Our human thinking is flawed, and we all have blind spots. Even pastors and seminary professors make mistakes in their thinking. That is why the Bible tells us:

> "Trust in the LORD with all thine heart; and lean not unto thine own understanding. In all thy ways acknowledge him, and he shall direct thy paths. Be not wise in thine own eyes: fear the LORD, and depart from evil." (Proverbs 3:5-7)

Our understanding is valuable, but it has limitations. We are children of God. Our heavenly Father knows everything. However, since we are "children," we are limited in our comprehension. We all make mistakes. The only man who ever got everything right was the Lord Jesus Christ.

Even the Apostle Paul had limitations in his understanding. He wrote nearly a fourth of the New Testament, and much of our theology is based on his writings, but he said:

> "For now we see through a glass darkly; but then face to face: **now I know in part**; but then shall I know even as also I am known." (1 Corinthians 13:12, emphasis added)

Paul said that he only knew "in part." He didn't fully comprehend everything. If Paul's understanding was incomplete, then modern Christians (who depend on Paul's writings) are even more limited in their understanding.

Therefore, we cannot have unquestioning confidence in any denomination, or church, or pastor, or teacher. We must test **everything** against what the Bible says. We need to do our own praying, and our own Bible studying, instead of relying on "experts" to do it for us.

Having a church and a pastor is valuable, and we should treasure them, but we need to be able to stand on our own if necessary. Even with a good church and a good pastor, we need to test everything that we are taught against Scripture. Good pastors can change. Sometimes all it takes is attending one conference or reading one book. The Bible warns us:

"Cursed be the man that trusteth in man, and maketh flesh his arm, and whose heart departeth from the LORD." (Jeremiah 17:5)

When the disciples asked Jesus what the signs of His return would be, the very first thing that He said was:

"Take heed that no man deceive you." (Matthew 24:4)

Today, there are some pastors who openly deny the Resurrection of Jesus Christ. My city has a large Baptist church whose pastor denies the Atonement (that Jesus died to save us from our sins). Some of these heretics have large, prosperous churches, so they probably have charismatic personalities. Their preaching probably sounds good to people who don't really think about what has been said, or who haven't read enough of the Bible to recognize when statements are contrary to Scripture.

There are even some pastors who don't believe in God. There are so many atheist pastors that they have an online support group. Their motto is "Moving beyond faith."[1]

The fact that such men can be pastors is amazing. Why don't the members of their churches recognize that something is seriously wrong, and either get rid of those pastors or else leave those churches?

We need to be on guard, because the devil wants to undermine our faith. The Bible warns us:

> "Be sober, be vigilant; because your adversary the devil, as a roaring lion, walketh about, seeking whom he may devour." (1 Peter 5:8)

Will we take a stand for true Christian doctrine, even if our family and our friends mock us because of it? And even if our pastor says that we are wrong?

Will we take a stand for Biblical standards of morality, even if the world calls it "hate speech"? Or if it is called a "hate crime" for which we can go to jail?

Where do our priorities lie? The Bible warns us against compromising our faith because of the fear of what men may do to us. Jesus told us:

> "And fear not them which kill the body, but are not able to kill the soul: but rather fear him which is able to destroy both soul and body in hell." (Matthew 10:28)

This is where the "fear of the Lord" becomes important. Our actions and attitudes have eternal consequences. Therefore, we need to have a healthy fear of God.

These days, it is popular to say that the "fear of the Lord" just means reverence. Well, it includes reverence, but it means more than that. God is our Judge, and He can send us to hell.

Jesus warned us that some people who think that they are good Christians will wind up in hell. He said:

"Not every one that saith unto me, Lord, Lord, shall enter into the kingdom of heaven; but he that doeth the will of my Father which is in heaven. Many will say to me in that day, Lord, Lord, have we not prophesied in thy name? and in thy name have cast out devils? and in thy name done many wonderful works? And then will I profess unto them, I never knew you: depart from me, ye that work iniquity." (Matthew 7:21-23)

Jesus also warned us that following Him would result in suffering. Some people react to hardship by getting angry at God and turning away from Him. Jesus told us:

"And he said to them all, If any man will come after me, let him deny himself, and take up his cross daily, and follow me." (Luke 9:23)

"And blessed is he, whosoever shall not be offended in me." (Luke 7:23)

Sometimes people become offended with God when they don't understand what God is doing. The Bible gives us an example of that:

"Many therefore of his disciples, when they had heard this, said, This is an hard saying; who can hear it? When Jesus knew in himself that his disciples murmured at it, he said unto them, Doth this offend you?... From that time many of his disciples went back, and walked no more with him. Then said Jesus unto the twelve, Will ye also go away? Then Simon Peter answered him, Lord, to whom shall we go? thou hast the words of eternal life." (John 6:60-61, 66-68)

Persecution is increasing. "Unthinkable" things are happening in the world today. When the pain and the sorrow come, will we turn **to** God? Or will we turn away from Him?

If things happen that we cannot understand, will we become offended with God?

If things turn out differently than we expected, based on what our pastor or our Sunday school teacher told us, will we say that the Bible isn't true? Will we call God a liar? Or will we say that our pastor or Sunday school teacher was mistaken?

Will we be like the disciples who became offended with Jesus and "walked no more with him"? Or will we be like Peter, who stuck with Jesus in spite of everything?

That's the bottom line, and our eternal destiny depends on what we do then.

Heaven and hell are very real. There is far more at stake than we can comprehend now. We won't fully understand it until we see Jesus face to face.

CHOOSE LIFE
(by Maria Kneas)

God sets before you life and death.
Choose life.

Jesus is the Way, the Truth and the Life.
The devil is a liar and a thief.
He wants to kill your hope and steal your joy
And fill your days with endless grief.

Jesus came to give unshakeable peace
And the only freedom that's real.
He wants to fill your heart with everlasting joy.
He wants to love and bless and heal.

God sets before you life and death.
Choose life.

Chapter 13

Renewing Our Minds

"And be not conformed to this world: but be ye transformed by the renewing of your mind" (Romans 12:2)

The Bible tells us to learn to think Biblically instead of thinking the way that the world does. The theme of transformation runs throughout the New Testament. God does not want us to stay where we are. He wants us to change—radically. Change is often difficult and can be painful. But it is what God wants and expects of us.

A Radical Transformation

God expects that, when we accept Jesus Christ as our Lord and Savior, we will be radically changed, transformed. The Greek word is *metamorphoo*. This transformation is to be a metamorphosis, of a magnitude at least comparable to that by which a caterpillar becomes a butterfly. God expects us to become totally different.

The Bible uses many different images to express the change that should occur:

- We become "a new creature: old things are passed away; behold, all things are become new." (2 Corinthians 5:17) We really become a new species. The Bible speaks of the first Adam who was earthly and fell into sin, and the second Adam (Jesus Christ) who was sinless and holy. It says that we will bear the likeness of the second Adam. (1 Corinthians 15:44-49

- "But we all, with open [unveiled] face beholding as in a glass [mirror] the glory of the Lord, are changed into the same image from glory to glory, even as by the Spirit of the Lord." (2 Corinthians 3:18)

- We are to be "renewed in the spirit of [our] mind" (Ephesians 4:23).

- We "put off... the old man" and "put on the new man." (Ephesians 4:22, 24)

- We live by the Spirit and not by the flesh. (Galatians 5:16; Romans 8:13)

- We become "instruments of righteousness" rather than "instruments of unrighteousness." (Romans 6:13)

- We have "been buried with him by baptism into death" in order that we may "walk in newness of life." (Romans 6:4)

- "I am crucified with Christ: nevertheless I live; yet not I, but Christ liveth in me." (Galatians 2:20)

- We have "been made free from sin" and have "become servants to God." (Romans 6:22) We are no longer servants "of sin unto death," but have become servants "of obedience unto righteousness" (Romans 6:16).

- God has "delivered us from the power of darkness, and hath translated us into the kingdom of his dear Son." (Colossians 1:13) Our citizenship and our allegiance have been changed.

- We have become adopted children of God. (John 1:12-13; Romans 8:15-16)

- We are born again; born from above, of the spirit and not the flesh. (John 3:3, 5)

Each of these images, in a different way, emphasizes the magnitude of the change that is expected. Each is dramatic and astonishing in itself. Their cumulative effect is even more powerful. We are talking about a tremendous transformation. It should be visible to others, but its internal effect should be far greater than what others can perceive.

If a person is not significantly changed by their salvation, then we are entitled to wonder whether their salvation was genuine. We are supposed to be salt and light to the world, and to let our light shine before men:

> "Ye are the salt of the earth: but if the salt have lost his savour, wherewith shall it be salted? it is thenceforth good for nothing, but to be cast out, and to be trodden under foot of men. Ye are the light of the world. A city that is set on an hill cannot be hid. Neither do men light a candle, and put it under a bushel, but on a candlestick; and it giveth light unto all that are in the house. Let your light so shine before men, that they may see your good works, and glorify your Father which is in heaven." (Matthew 5:13-16)

We need to live in such a way that the difference between Christians and non-Christians is inescapable. We need to stand, boldly and clearly, for what we believe.

The Fruit of Transformation

What is the result of this metamorphosis? The Bible states it in a number of different ways, which overlap and can be seen as different ways of expressing the same basic concept. The Bible often does this, because our minds are inadequate to comprehend—and our language inadequate to express—the full scope of God's revelation to us.

Developing Godly Character

The whole concept can be summed up by saying that our character is to become more and more like God's character. We are to "put on the new man, which after God is created in righteousness and true holiness." (Ephesians 4:24)

> "…ye have put off the old man with his deeds; And have put on the new man, which is renewed in knowledge after the image of him that created him" (Colossians 3:9-10)

God intends us "to be conformed to the image of his Son." (Romans 8:29) We are supposed to think more and more like Jesus Christ does. (1 Corinthians 2:16)

There are some other Biblical ways of expressing the same concept.

Living for the Things that are Unseen

Two of the great statements about this transformation are:

> "But we all, with open [unveiled] face beholding as in a glass [mirror] the glory of the Lord, are changed into the same image from glory to glory, even as by the Spirit of the Lord." (2 Corinthians 3:18)

"Therefore if any man be in Christ, he is a new creature: old things are passed away; behold, all things are become new" (2 Corinthians 5:17)

A look at what is said between those two statements tells us a good deal about the nature of this transformation.

In 2 Corinthians, chapters 4 and 5, Paul repeatedly contrasts the material world in which our bodies now live, and the spiritual world. He tells us that the spiritual world is the real one, on which we should focus. He says that we should not regard people from a worldly point of view ("after the flesh"). (2 Corinthians 5:16) And he points out that the man without the Spirit cannot understand spiritual things. Paul said,

"...the god of this world hath blinded the minds of them which believe not, lest the light of the glorious gospel of Christ, who is the image of God, should shine unto them" (2 Corinthians 4:4)

"But the natural man receiveth not the things of the Spirit of God: for they are foolishness unto him: neither can he know them, because they are spiritually discerned." (1 Corinthians 2:14)

"While we look not at the things which are seen, but at the things which are not seen: for the things which are seen are temporal; but the things which are not seen are eternal." (2 Corinthians 4:18)

"For we walk by faith, not by sight." (2 Corinthians 5:7)

"Now faith is the substance of things hoped for, the evidence of things not seen." (Hebrews 11:1)

> "If ye then be risen with Christ, seek those things which are above, where Christ sitteth on the right hand of God. Set your affection on things above, not on things on the earth." (Colossians 3:1-2)

God is spirit and he lives primarily in the realm of the spirit. He lived in that realm before there was any physical universe, and he will live in it even though heaven and earth pass away. (See Isaiah 51:6.)

We need to learn to see things from God's perspective. This results in a wholly different order of priorities.

First, the natural person, the untransformed person, lives primarily for material things. His priorities are those of the material world.

In contrast, the transformed person lives primarily in a spiritual world. He lives primarily by faith in God and in God's word, rather than by his physical senses. He regards the unseen things of faith as more real and more lasting than the material things which surround him. The transformed person is living primarily in a different world, a world in which spiritual rather than material things have primary importance.

Second, where the natural person lives only for this life, the transformed person is already living in Eternity. Paul speaks of this in many ways. For Paul, tribulations and difficulties of this world become minor when compared to the glory to come. Paul says,

> "For which cause we faint not; but though our outward man perish, yet the inward man is renewed day by day. For our light affliction, which is but for a moment, worketh for us a far more exceeding and eternal weight of glory." (2 Corinthians 4:16-17)

> "Beloved, think it not strange concerning the fiery trial which is to try you, as though some strange thing

happened unto you: But rejoice, inasmuch as ye are partakers of Christ's sufferings; that, when his glory shall be revealed, ye may be glad also with exceeding joy." (1 Peter 4:12-13)

Paul says that Christians can be confident, because we know that when we leave this earthly body, then we will be with the Lord. (2 Corinthians 5:6) Of course, that is a wonderful thing.

Jesus warned us that in this world we will face hard times. But He also assured us that we can be at peace, in spite of it, because of Him.

"These things I have spoken unto you, that in me ye might have peace. In the world ye shall have tribulation: but be of good cheer; I have overcome the world." (John 16:33)

Paul warned us that we should expect to face difficulties. Having to endure such things is a normal part of Christian life.

"Confirming the souls of the disciples, and exhorting them to continue in the faith, and that **we must through much tribulation enter into the kingdom of God**." (Acts 14:22, emphasis added)

"Yea, and all that will live godly in Christ Jesus shall suffer persecution." (2 Timothy 3:12)

However, we can rejoice in spite our troubles (and even in the midst of them), because we learn and grow from them, and because the glory that is to come is far greater than our troubles are. God can make ALL things work out for our long-term, eternal good. No exceptions.

"My brethren, count it all joy when ye fall into divers temptations; Knowing this, that the trying of your faith worketh patience. But let patience have her perfect work, that ye may be perfect and entire, wanting nothing." (James 1:2-4)

"And not only so, but we glory in tribulations also: knowing that tribulation worketh patience; And patience, experience; and experience, hope: And hope maketh not ashamed; because the love of God is shed abroad in our hearts by the Holy Ghost which is given unto us." (Romans 5:3-5)

"And we know that all things work together for good to them that love God, to them who are the called according to his purpose." (Romans 8:28)

Third, those who live should no longer live for themselves, but for Jesus, who died for us. (2 Corinthians 5:15) Therefore, we should make it our goal to please Him. (2 Corinthians 5:9) We should not be like those who want to please men more than they want to please God. (John 12:43) Jesus told us,

"If the world hate you, ye know that it hated me before it hated you. If ye were of the world, the world would love his own: but because ye are not of the world, but I have chosen you out of the world, therefore the world hateth you." (John 15:18-19)

These are all major shifts in our attitudes and priorities. Truly they require a renewing of the mind.

Living by the Spirit

When we receive Jesus Christ as our Lord and Savior, God sends us the Holy Spirit to live with us and be in us. (John 14:16) It is because we have the Holy Spirit living in us, and His power working in us, that we are able to be transformed. But the process is not instantaneous. The Holy Spirit inhabits our spirit, but our soul and body need to be brought under the Spirit's control.

Becoming Yielded to God

Part of what living by the Spirit means is that we are wholly yielded to God. We are no longer servants of sin, but servants of obedience and righteousness. (Romans 6:16) We submit ourselves to God. (James 4:7)

The Process of Transformation

This transformation is a process. It does not happen all at once. We are transformed into His likeness with glory that keeps increasing. (2 Corinthians 3:18)

We spend a lifetime learning how to live by the Spirit, to live a new life. We must keep making every effort to be holy. (Hebrews 12:14) We must submit, and keep on submitting, to God. Over and over and over we must take our thoughts captive to obey Christ. (2 Corinthians 10:5) Near the end of his life, Paul did not consider that he had arrived. (Philippians 3:12)

One aspect of this transformation is showing the "fruit of the spirit." A farmer cannot cause fruit to grow. However, he can create conditions that are favorable to its growth.

In somewhat the same way, we cannot cause God's character to grow within us. Only God can do that. But we can create favorable conditions for its growth—by faith, prayer, Bible study, and guarding our thoughts.

Believe

We need to believe that God can, and will, transform us into His image—that this astonishing metamorphosis can, and will, occur.

We need to consider Him faithful who has made the promise. (Hebrews 11:11)

Choose

We must make an act of the will. We must choose to be transformed, choose to put off the old self and put on the new self, choose to live by the Spirit, choose to submit to God, choose to be weapons of righteousness, etc.

Stay in God's Word

The agent that renews our mind is the Word of God. It is not enough just to read the Bible. We need to believe it, take it seriously, and follow it. We need to let it dwell in us, work in us, become engrafted in us, become a part of us.

The Bible speaks often about the importance of meditating on the Word of God. (Joshua 1:8; Psalms 1:2, 119:78) The Hebrew word for "meditate" suggests a cow chewing its cud, working the material over and over to extract all the good from it.

Guard Our Thoughts

If we would be transformed by the renewing of our mind—be made new in the attitude of our mind—we need to carefully guard what goes into our mind. We need to think on those things that are true, noble, right, pure, etc. (Philippians 4:8) Even more important, we need to guard against our own wrong thoughts—the thoughts that come from the flesh and not the spirit.

We need to take our thoughts captive to obey Christ. (2 Corinthians 10:5) We need to do this, not just daily, but moment by moment. Whenever we find ourselves thinking thoughts that are contrary to what the Bible says, we need to repudiate them, renounce them, and replace them with thoughts that are Biblically true.

Pray

We need to pray for wisdom and for any other quality that we lack.

> "If any of you lack wisdom, let him ask of God, that giveth to all men liberally, and upbraideth not; and it shall be given him." (James 1:5)

> "Ask, and it shall be given you; seek, and ye shall find; knock, and it shall be opened unto you" (Matthew 7:7)

The form of the verbs means "keep on asking," "keep on seeking," "keep on knocking." When we keep asking God to change us into His likeness, we unite our will with His and cooperate with His work in our lives.

Persevere

Jesus told His disciples to persist in prayer. (Luke 18:1-7, 11:5-10) We are to "run with patience the race that is set before us." (Hebrews 12:1)

The Bible is full of words telling us to apply ourselves diligently to the task before us. We need to keep pursuing, making every effort, pressing on, continuing, standing, etc.

If ye then be risen with Christ,
seek those things which are above,
where Christ sitteth on the right hand of God.
Set your affection on things above,
not on things on the earth.
(Colossians 3:1-2)

Rejoice in the Lord alway; and again I say, Rejoice;
Let your moderation be know unto all men.
The Lord is at hand.
Be careful [anxious] for nothing;
but in every thing
by prayer and suplication with thanksgiving
let your requests be made known unto God.
And the peace of God,
which passeth all understanding,
shall keep your hearts and minds
through Christ Jesus.
(Philippians 4:4-7)

Finally, brethren,
whatsoever things are true,
whatsoever things are honest,
whatsoever things are just,
whatsoever things are pure,
whatsoever things are lovely,
whatsoever things are of good report;
if there be any virtue,
and if there be any praise,
think on these things.
(Philippians 4:8)

Chapter 14

Building Faith

> *"But ye, beloved, **building up yourselves on your most holy faith**, praying in the Holy Ghost, Keep yourselves in the love of God, looking for the mercy of our Lord Jesus Christ unto eternal life."* (Jude 1:20-21, emphasis added)

The best way to build up our faith is to obey God. When we obey Him, then we grow in our understanding of Him, and we learn to trust Him more. That makes it easier for us to obey Him. It's a good cycle.

In order to obey God, we need to develop a working knowledge of the Bible, because that is where God tells us what He is like and how He wants us to live. If we have a church with good, Biblical preaching, that is a wonderful blessing. However, we cannot depend on our pastor. We need to know the Bible ourselves.

Persecution is increasing world-wide. In America, we are in the early stages of persecution, and it is getting worse. If it becomes full blown, then we may not be able to have a Bible. Therefore, we need to get the Word of God inside us now—while we still can.

We can no longer take having Bibles for granted, or being able to go to church. A time may come when even meeting with a few friends to pray and talk about Scripture will become dangerous. Jesus warned us:

> "Then shall they deliver you up to be afflicted, and shall kill you: and ye shall be hated of all nations for my name's sake. And then shall many be offended, and shall betray

one another, and shall hate one another." (Matthew 24:9-10)

I have friends who have been memorizing Scripture for years for that very reason. Some also memorize hymns and worship songs, so that they can sing them silently, in their head. That is what the Bible calls "making melody in your heart to the Lord." (Ephesians 5:19)

When we read the Bible, it is good to ask God to give us understanding. He wrote it by having the Holy Spirit show various human authors what to say and how to say it. God knows what the Scriptures mean, and He can open our eyes and our hearts to the Truth in the Bible.

There are some things that we can't really understand now, but God will give us the understanding if and when we need it. For example, there are some things in the Book of Revelation that will become very clear to the Christians who are alive when those events occur. They will be able to say, "Oh, so that's what God meant!"

We see an example of that in the Gospels when they say that certain events fulfilled specific prophecies. At the time that the prophets wrote those prophecies, they didn't understand what it was about. Hundreds of years later, when those prophecies were fulfilled, then it became clear.

Another way to build faith is praise and worship. The Bible says that God "inhabits" our praise. (Psalm 22:3) I don't understand that intellectually, but it implies that when we worship, there is a kind of closeness to God that we don't have otherwise.

Paul said that Christ is **in** us. (Colossians 1:27) You can't get any closer than that. So it may be that what worship does is to make us more aware of God's presence, to make us more sensitive to Him. We can become so preoccupied with the cares of daily life that we tune God out. Then, when we worship, we get our focus back, and become more aware of Him.

Another way to build our faith is through prayer. Again, that makes us more aware of God. It gets us tuned in to Him. It reminds us of His love and His faithfulness, and how He takes care of us and those we love.

When we see answers to prayer, that increases our faith. However, if we don't see an answer to prayer, that should not discourage us. God may be working behind the scenes in a way that we don't understand. Or it may be that we are not praying according to His will, that what we want would not be good for us or for those we are praying for.

God sees the big picture. We don't. Our human understanding is very limited.

Children often ask their parents for things that would not be good for them. For example, many young boys want to drive the family car, but the results would be disastrous because they don't have the judgment, skill, or maturity to do it safely. However, they don't understand that. When parents refuse such requests, it's because they love their children and don't want them to get hurt. Well, God is the same way with us.

One thing that can increase our love for God (which increases our faith in Him) is to go through some of the things that Jesus suffered. Paul said:

"That I may know him, and the power of his resurrection, and the fellowship of his sufferings, being made conformable unto his death" (Philippians 3:10)

For example, have you ever done something good, and had people misunderstand you, criticize you for it, or even punish you for doing the right thing? If so, then that will give you some understanding of what Jesus went through His entire life. When He healed people out of love and compassion, the pharisees wanted to kill Him because of it. Eventually, they were able to get Him crucified.

What we suffer is small compared to what Jesus endured, but it can help us know Him better and love Him more. It gives us more reasons to be grateful to Him, because it gives us some understanding of how much He was willing to go through in order to save us.

One way to get to know God better is by studying Scripture. There are some good resources that can help us understand the Bible better. The *Henry Morris Study Bible* is quite helpful. (It used to be called *The Defender's Study Bible*, but after Dr. Morris died, it was renamed in his honor, since he wrote the notes for it.)

There are many so-called "experts" who are trying to undermine our faith. One tactic of such people is to engage in what they call "higher criticism." Perhaps a more accurate term for it would be, "trying to find intellectual excuses for not believing the Bible." Their theories forget something that is very important and should be obvious—the Bible tells us about **real** people in real life.

For example, these "scholars" analyze the vocabulary in Paul's epistles, and say that some of them must have a different author because the writing style and vocabulary are different. Well, in real life, people write differently based on who they are writing to and what they are writing about.

If those scholars analyzed the chapters that I wrote in this book, they would conclude that there were two authors, one who writes about Scripture, and another who writes about current events, using a different style and vocabulary. And they would attribute my poems to a third author. However, I can assure you that I am only one person.

Think about your own life. Would you write to your boss the same way that you would write to your spouse or your children? Would you write a love letter the same way that you write business correspondence? Of course not. These so-called "experts" have lost their common sense.

Such "scholars" also analyze the parables of Jesus, as presented in the Gospels, and make a big deal out of the fact that there are variations in the stories. They have forgotten something. Jesus was a real man, living a real life. The Bible shows Him constantly on the move, teaching in many places. In real life, traveling preachers tell the same stories many times, with variations in how they tell them.

Think about stories that are told in your own family. How many times have you heard your mother or father tell somebody about something that you did as a child? Every time, the story is a little different. That's because they are talking about something real, as opposed to reciting something that they memorized.

Some "experts" also make a big deal out of the fact that two Gospels tell about blind Bartimaeus by himself, and one Gospel mentions two blind men, instead of just talking about Bartimaeus. If you were a blind beggar, wouldn't you hang out with other blind beggars? You would have a lot in common. They would understand you in a way that the rest of the world doesn't. So Bartimaeus was with a blind friend, and two Gospels just mention him, but the other Gospel mentions his friend as well. That is not a problem.

In real life, if several people witness the same event and write accounts about it, there is variation in the stories, because different people focus on different aspects of what happened. For example, were you ever with family members or friends when something notable happened, and then afterwards you heard different people talk about the event? Don't they emphasize different things? One person may major on something that another person doesn't even mention. That is what happens in everyday life.

If so-called "experts" give you sophisticated-sounding reasons for not believing what the Bible says, please don't let them undermine your faith. I'm speaking from personal experience. When I first came to know the Lord, I loved the Bible so much that I went to a college that claimed to be Christian, and I majored in religion. My professors filled my head with that kind of nonsense. It destroyed my trust in Scripture and almost shipwrecked my faith in God. It took me many years to recover from that.

God brought the right people into my life. He also led me to the right books. I saw archaeological evidence that confirms what the Bible says, and ways that Biblical prophecies have been fulfilled in history.

Here is something that helped restore my trust in Scripture. Sir William Ramsay is an archaeologist who spent years researching the historical statements made by the Apostle Luke in the Book of Acts. He even sailed the route that Paul sailed in order to test the accuracy of Luke's nautical statements. Ramsay wrote:

> "Further study… showed that the book [Acts] could bear the most minute scrutiny as an authority for the facts of the Aegean world." [1]

> "You may press the words of Luke in a degree beyond any other historian's and they stand the keenest scrutiny and the hardest treatment." [2]

> "Acts may justly be quoted as a trustworthy historical authority." [3]

> "Luke is a historian of the first rank." [4]

Getting to know God is a lifetime adventure, and the Bible is amazing. Many times I have read a familiar passage, and all at once it seemed to jump off the page at me. Suddenly I understood it in a way that I never saw it before. That is the Holy Spirit working in us:

> "But the Comforter, which is the Holy Ghost, whom the Father will send in my name, **he shall teach you all things,** and bring all things to your remembrance,

whatsoever I have said unto you." (John 14:26, emphasis added)

Jesus promised that He would always be with us. That includes helping us get to know Him better and love Him more. It also includes guiding us and enabling us to be faithful to Him:

"Go ye therefore, and teach all nations, baptizing them in the name of the Father, and of the Son, and of the Holy Ghost: Teaching them to observe all things whatsoever I have commanded you: and, **lo, I am with you always, even unto the end of the world**." (Matthew 28:19-20, emphasis added)

"Let your conversation be without covetousness; and be content with such things as ye have: for he hath said, **I will never leave thee, nor forsake thee**." (Hebrews 13:5, emphasis added)

THOU HIDDEN SOURCE OF CALM REPOSE
(by Charles Wesley, 1749)

Jesus, my all in all Thou art:
My rest in toil, my ease in pain,
The medicine of my broken heart;
In war my peace, in loss my gain,
My smile beneath the tyrant's frown
In shame my glory and my crown;

In want my plentiful supply,
In weakness my almighty power;
In bonds my perfect liberty,
My light in Satan's darkest hour;
My joy in grief, my shield in strife,
In death my everlasting life.

(Public domain)

Chapter 15

Learning To Trust God More

"O taste and see that the Lord is good: blessed is the man that trusteth in him." (Psalm 34:8)

In order to learn to trust someone, you have to get to know them better. That includes spending time with them, and communicating with them. When it comes to God, we communicate through prayer and worship, and we learn about Him by reading the Bible, where He tells us a lot about Himself, and we see him act in the lives of His people.

I also find it helpful to read books about the lives of great men and women of faith. One of my favorites is Gladys Aylward, a missionary to China who had amazing adventures there, including taking a hundred children over the mountains to safety during the Japanese invasion of China. She was even able to reach the local Mandarin, who gave up his many wives and became a Christian. (A good biography is *The Small Woman*.) Another is Eric Liddell, the Olympic runner who became a missionary to China. (A good biography is *Complete Surrender*.)

Corrie ten Boom is one of my heroes. *The Hiding Place* tells of her family's work with the Dutch Underground during the Nazi occupation of Holland. They smuggled Jews to safe places and hid Jews in their home. Eventually they were betrayed and sent to a German concentration camp. I recommend reading the book and getting the DVD. The book has a lot more information than you can put into a movie, but the movie enables you to see things in action. Corrie was there as a consultant when they made the movie, so it is very accurate. Knowing Corrie, she was praying all the time while the movie was being produced.

In My Father's House tells of their life before the war; how as a family, they had strong faith and regular prayer and Bible study, and the many ways that they reached out to others. Among other things, Corrie led a Bible study for mentally retarded children. After the war, Corrie wrote many books, and I have probably read them all. She talked so much about God's love and the ways that He comes through for His people, giving many beautiful examples from her own life and from the lives of people she touched. There are three quotations from Corrie that I often think about. They are:

"Never be afraid to trust an unknown future to a known God."

"There is no pit so deep that He is not deeper still."

"Worry does not deprive tomorrow of its sorrow. It deprives today of its strength."

Some Christians have found my book *How to Fight Discouragement* to be quite helpful. I wrote it because the threat of persecution is discouraging. Since then I've discovered that the book is also helping Christians who have health problems and other kinds of difficulties.

All of us have blind spots and areas where our understanding is flawed or inadequate. The most important thing is whether or not we have a heart for God.

When we see Jesus face to face, the mistakes in our thinking will immediately disappear. The big question is, will we hear Him say, "Well done, thou good and faithful servant"? And that depends on our hearts.

Here is an example from everyday life. Suppose a family has small children and a flower garden, and a young child picks some of those flowers to give to his mother, because he loves her and wants to please her. Would a loving mother be delighted by this show of love? Or would she scold him for messing up the flower garden?

Sometimes we do things for God in ways that are comparable. We want to show love and do something for Him, but we don't have enough understanding to be able to take all of the factors into account.

When I was a little girl, I used to ask my Mom if I could "holp" her cook dinner. Of course she said "yes," even though it meant that there would be spills and messes, and it would take more time and trouble to make dinner than if she did it by herself. Sometimes when we are serving God we are like I was as a little girl, "holping" in the kitchen. We make messes because we don't know how to do things. That is part of the learning process.

My Mom was happy when I "holped" her, and God likes it when we "holp" Him, too. And for the same reason. Love. While we are "holping," we are building relationship and learning.

Compared to God, we are just toddlers. If we can see ourselves and others as being like young children who are learning, then we can have more patience when we (or they) make mistakes. This perspective also makes it easier to forgive.

Our understanding is valuable, but (as with little children) it is inadequate. The Bible says:

> "Trust in the Lord with all thine heart; and lean not unto thine own understanding. In all thy ways acknowledge him, and he shall direct thy paths. Be not wise in thine own eyes: fear the Lord, and depart from evil." (Proverbs 3:5-7)

We do have some degree of understanding. We should use what we have and be grateful for it. However, we cannot put all of our weight on it, because it is inadequate. Like little children, we don't see the big picture and we don't understand our own limitations. Our Father in Heaven does. So we need to lean on Him all the time.

Our primary trust needs to be in God Himself, as opposed to our understanding of Him and of the world. The Apostle Paul made this quite clear. He said:

> "For the which cause I also suffer these things: nevertheless I am not ashamed: for I know **whom** I have believed, and am persuaded that he is able to keep that which I have committed unto him against that day." (2 Timothy 1:12, emphasis added)

Notice that Paul said "**whom**," which means a person, namely God. He did not say "what," which would be a system of theology, interpretation of Scripture, his understanding of the world, and things like that. Paul's trust was in Almighty God—not in his own ability to figure things out.

Paul had an amazing experience, a revelation of Heaven. He saw and heard things that he was not allowed to tell us about:

> "I knew a man in Christ above fourteen years ago, (whether in the body, I cannot tell; or whether out of the body, I cannot tell: God knoweth;) such an one caught up to the third heaven. And I knew such a man, (whether in the body, or out of the body, I cannot tell: God knoweth;) How that he was caught up into paradise, and heard unspeakable words, which it is not lawful for a man to utter." (2 Corinthians 12:2-4)

However, Paul's trust was not in this experience or in those revelations. It was in Almighty God. He trusted a person (God) rather than his own experiences in Heaven. He openly told us that he only knew "in part," that his understanding was limited:

> "For **we know in part**, and we prophesy in part." (1 Corinthians 13:9, emphasis added)

"For now we see through a glass, darkly; but then face to face: now **I know in part**; but then shall I know even as also I am known." (1 Corinthians 13:12, emphasis added)

Paul was like a little boy who knows that everything is going to be alright because Daddy is with him, and Daddy knows how to take care of things. And that's the way that we need to be. That may be one of the things that Jesus meant when He used the term "poor in spirit." He told us that we should come to God like little children:

"Blessed are the poor in spirit: for theirs is the kingdom of heaven." (Matthew 5:3)

"Verily I say unto you, Except ye be converted, and become as little children, ye shall not enter into the kingdom of heaven." (Matthew 18:3)

That kind of humility and conscious dependance on God goes against the grain. Being fallen creatures who are sinful by nature, we want to think that we have it all together and we know what we are doing. Well, that is partly true, but only partly. At our best, we are clumsy, and at times all of us become what the Bible calls "stiff necked" (stubborn and rebellious). That goes along with our sinful nature.

Even the best Christian is still just a sinner saved by grace. None of us will be fully right until we see Jesus face to face. And what a wonderful day that will be! The Apostle John said:

"Beloved, now are we the sons of God, and it doth not yet appear what we shall be: but we know that, when he shall appear, we shall be like him; for we shall see him as he is." (1 John 3:2)

Paul said something that sounds very strange. I've wondered about it for years. I think I understand some aspects of it, but there is probably a lot more gold in this mine that I haven't found yet. Paul said:

> "That I may know him, and the power of his resurrection, and the **fellowship of his sufferings**, being made conformable unto his death" (Philippians 3:10, emphasis added)

I can see why Paul wanted to know the power of Jesus' resurrection. But why would Paul want to know (or experience) the sufferings that Jesus went through? Or to somehow share in them?

Soldiers on the front lines go through traumatic things together. They share in the same sufferings, and sometimes they save one another's lives. There is a kind of bond that soldiers can build with their battle buddies that cannot be developed under other circumstances. There is a closeness, a loyalty, and a willingness to lay down their lives for one another.

I remember reading about a battle during World War II when our troops were trapped, hemmed in by barbed wire, which made them sitting ducks—trapped and waiting to be killed by the Germans. Immediately, some of the soldiers ran full speed into that barbed wire, impaling themselves on it. That enabled the other soldiers to climb up over the barbed wire on the backs of their battle buddies. I cannot imagine the level of courage and dedication and loyalty and love that would be required to do something like that.

When we endure some of things that Jesus went through, to some extent that makes us become His battle buddy. It builds a relationship between us that cannot be built any other way.

It also gives us some idea of how much He was willing to suffer for us. What we go through is small compared to what Jesus suffered, but it is similar. A man with a broken foot has more understanding of what soldiers with amputated legs go through than a healthy runner does.

As we learn more about what Jesus was willing to go through in order to save us, we have more reasons to be grateful to Him, and it increases our trust in Him. If He loved us enough to suffer like that for us, then we can trust Him to do what is best for us.

Another thing that increases our trust is when we see God protect us. For example, one time I was at a stop light in front of a curved suspension bridge. Its curve was so high that I couldn't see what was on the other side of the bridge. I was in the left turn lane, waiting for the arrow to make my turn. When I got the green arrow, I started to turn. But then somehow I felt that I should not move, that I needed to stay there. So I did. And a few seconds later, a big truck came barreling down the bridge. He must have run the red light on the other side of the bridge. If I had made my turn when the green arrow came on, I would have been right in his path. I would have been crushed by that big truck.

That is one time when God saved my life and I am aware of it. How many other times has God rescued me when I wasn't aware of it? I won't find out until I get to Heaven.

Another thing that builds trust is when we are cornered, we have our back to the wall, and if God doesn't come through for us, then we have had it. Then God does come through. He rescues us, and that teaches us to trust Him more.

For example, I used to work in a neighborhood that was dangerous at night. Because I didn't have a car, I had to take a bus to get home. One day, my job required me to work so late that it was very dark when I left the office. The street was deserted, except for one man. As soon as he noticed me, he headed in my direction. That did not look good. Since he was between me and the office building, I couldn't run back to the office for refuge.

That man came closer and closer, and I became more and more frightened. Just then, a man walked out of my office building and came straight towards us, walking quickly. I think he probably noticed my perilous situation. As soon as he got near us, the other man ran away. The man from the office stayed with me until my bus arrived.

That was close timing, and I believe that God was behind it. He can "nudge" people to do things. He has ways of getting people where they need to be (like a sheep dog does with sheep). My Mom used to call that kind of thing "God's choreography." (God knows how to get people in the right place at the right time, and do it in complex ways when needed.)

You may ask, "What if that man had not rescued me? What if I had been raped?" Remember Romans 8:28. It includes **everything**—no exceptions:

> "And we know that **all** things work together for good to them that love God, to them who are the called according to his purpose." (Romans 8:28, emphasis added)

In the case of rape, there is another Scripture that applies. God brought this to my mind when I was praying with a friend who had been homosexually raped when he was five years old. In context, Jesus was talking about food. However, the principle applies to other things as well, including rape:

> "There is nothing from without a man, that entering into him can defile him" (Mark 7:15)

No matter what we go through, God is willing and able to heal our hearts and comfort us:

> "He healeth the broken in heart, and bindeth up their wounds." (Psalm 147:3)

> "For the Lamb which is in the midst of the throne shall feed them, and shall lead them unto living fountains of waters: and God shall wipe away all tears from their eyes." (Revelation 7:17)

In addition, there is an important principle that the Apostle Paul told us about:

> "Who comforteth us in all our tribulation, that we may be able to comfort them which are in any trouble, by the comfort wherewith we ourselves are comforted of God." (2 Corinthians 1:4)

When we go through bad things, God is able to heal us and comfort us. And then we are able to help and comfort others who go through similar things.

For example, I'm a widow. Because of that, I understand other widows in a way that women whose husbands are still alive can't do. It also gives me understanding of anybody who has had a death in the family, and I can comfort them in ways that other people can't do.

There was a time in communist Russia when Christians were severely persecuted. They endured great suffering, both physical and psychological. Those who were faithful to God became sweeter, more gentle, and more devoted. They came closer to God, instead of becoming bitter and turning away from Him. (The biography *A Small Price to Pay* tells about one family which went through that.) I've heard similar stories about persecuted Christians in China.

Remember Shadrach, Mesach, and Abednego? They knew that God was able to deliver them, but their faithfulness did not depend on being rescued:

> "If it be so, our God whom we serve is able to deliver us from the burning fiery furnace, and he will deliver us out of thine hand, O king. But if not, be it known unto thee, O king, that we will not serve thy gods, nor worship the golden image which thou hast set up." (Daniel 3:17-18)

They knew that God had the power to save them, but they were determined to be faithful, even if it meant being burned alive. Their loyalty to God and their trust in Him did not depend on whether or not he rescued them from that situation. And that's the way that we need to be.

Hebrews 11 tells about men and women who had great faith. People like to read about miracles that God did for heroes of the faith such as Abraham and Moses. However, the last five verses tell of heroes who were tortured and martyred for their faith. The transition occurs in verse 35:

> "Women received their dead raised to life again: and others were tortured, not accepting deliverance; that they might obtain a better resurrection" (Hebrews 11:35)

When God miraculously heals somebody, or raises them from the dead, we admire His power and are grateful for His love. However, I suspect that it takes even more power for Him to enable a frail human being to endure being tortured to death, trusting in God while he goes through it, and praying for his persecutors instead of hating them. For example, Stephen prayed for the people who were stoning him to death, while they were doing it:

> "Then they cried out with a loud voice, and stopped their ears, and ran upon him with one accord, And cast him out of the city, and stoned him: and the witnesses laid down their clothes at a young man's feet, whose name was Saul. And they stoned Stephen, calling upon God, and saying, Lord Jesus, receive my spirit. And he kneeled down, and cried with a loud voice, Lord, lay not this sin to their charge. And when he had said this, he fell asleep." (Acts 7:57-60)

Prepare for Persecution

Notice that Saul (Paul) was there when this happened. I wonder if that contributed to his conversion. Since he was there at the time, Paul is one of the men that Stephen prayed for.

If we are able to avoid being harmed by others, without compromising our faith, then we should do so. Paul avoided a Roman whipping. He had been whipped by the Jews, but that was limited to 39 lashes. With the Romans, there was no limit, and some people died from those whippings. Here is how Paul avoided it by using Roman law:

> "The chief captain commanded him to be brought into the castle, and bade that he should be examined by scourging; that he might know wherefore they cried so against him. And as they bound him with thongs, Paul said unto the centurion that stood by, Is it lawful for you to scourge a man that is a Roman, and uncondemned? When the centurion heard that, he went and told the chief captain, saying, Take heed what thou doest: for this man is a Roman. Then the chief captain came, and said unto him, Tell me, art thou a Roman? He said, Yea. And the chief captain answered, With a great sum obtained I this freedom. And Paul said, But I was free born. Then straightway they departed from him which should have examined him: and the chief captain also was afraid, after he knew that he was a Roman, and because he had bound him." (Acts 22:24-29)

So we should be prudent and avoid unnecessary suffering. At the same time, if we do suffer, then we can look to see how Jesus went through similar things, and share in the "fellowship of his sufferings."

It's a win/win situation. It's good to avoid suffering and hardship if we can do so without denying God. However, if we go through it, then that will bring us closer to God, if we respond

Biblically. And that will increase our trust and faith in God, and our love for Him.

That brings me back to Romans 8:28, which is a verse that has had a profound influence on my life. We are never at the mercy of men or of circumstances, because God is willing and able to make **everything** work out for our long-term, eternal good, if we love Him. No exceptions:

> "And we know that all things work together for good to them that love God, to them who are the called according to his purpose." (Romans 8:28)

God gives us grace and blessing in His real world, in the present moment. If we get lost in the past (through regrets, or wishing we were back in "the good old days," or in other ways), we won't find God's blessing there. If we get lost in the future (through fears, or hopes, or wishful thinking), we won't find His grace there, either. And we won't find it when we are daydreaming or lost in some imaginary world.

When Corrie ten Boom was a little girl, she asked her Daddy what it was like to die. He replied by asking Corrie, "When we go to the train station, when do I give you your ticket?" She replied, "When I am getting on the train." Corrie's father used that example to teach her that God gives us His grace at the very moment that we need it—not ahead of time.

That's a good thing, because otherwise our trust would be in having "grace in the bank" instead of trusting in God Himself. Good parents want to develop and strengthen their relationship with their children, and our Father in Heaven does the same with His children.

God knows the right timing for things. He is always with us. He will never leave us, or forget us, or fail to take care of us. However, He often does it at the very last minute.

God will get us through whatever we have to go through. When it is all over, then He will comfort us and heal us. Some day we will be in Heaven, with Resurrection Bodies, and God will wipe away all our tears:

> "Can a woman forget her sucking child, that she should not have compassion on the son of her womb? yea, they may forget, yet will I not forget thee." (Isaiah 49:15)

> "And the ransomed of the Lord shall return, and come to Zion with songs and everlasting joy upon their heads: they shall obtain joy and gladness, and sorrow and sighing shall flee away." (Isaiah 35:10)

> "Go ye therefore, and teach all nations, baptizing them in the name of the Father, and of the Son, and of the Holy Ghost: Teaching them to observe all things whatsoever I have commanded you: and, **lo, I am with you always**, even unto the end of the world. Amen." (Matthew 28:19-20, emphasis added)

> "For the Lamb which is in the midst of the throne shall feed them, and shall lead them unto living fountains of waters: and God shall wipe away all tears from their eyes." (Revelation 7:17)

> "And God shall wipe away all tears from their eyes; and there shall be no more death, neither sorrow, nor crying, neither shall there be any more pain: for the former things are passed away. And he that sat upon the throne said, Behold, I make all things new." (Revelation 21:4-5)

BLEST
(by Frances Morrisson) (My Mom)

O be blessed,
    unruffled by clamorings of the past,
    by fears for what we hold most dear.

O be blessed,
    flowing by His spirit
    toward His image;
    flexing to His plans —
    whether shadowy or clear.

Be blessed this very moment,
the only time of touch or blessing:
    for the past has fled;
    but the future is not here.

Chapter 16

Do We Love God?

"Thou shalt love the LORD thy God with all thy heart, and with all thy soul, and with all thy mind." (Matthew 22:37)

Years ago I had a sweet conure named Alexander. (A conure is a bird about the size of a parrot.) It took him months to decide that he wanted to be my friend. But when he did, he was wholehearted about it. He would lick my face and groom my eyebrows. And when I scritched him and talked to him in a certain tone of voice, he would fluff his feathers from happiness. That little fella really loved me.

One time I came home from the hospital in pain from having had major surgery, and Alexander kept getting into my bed in order to try to comfort me. I didn't want to have bird poop in my bed, and I was afraid that I might fall asleep and roll over on him, so I kept calling Mom to have her take him and put him back on the perch on top of his cage. But as soon as Mom left, he would come right back. That birdie knew that I was in pain, and he was determined to comfort me.

In contrast, once I went to a pet store where they had baby cockatiels. Those sweet little birds were all over me, as if they loved me. But I quickly realized that it had nothing to do with love. They thought that I had some food for them. The difference between their behavior and that of Alexander was striking.

When I lived with my brother, when he came home at night both of his boys would eagerly run to the door shouting, "Daddy's home! Daddy's home!" And they would jump into his arms. Sometimes my brother had a piece of candy for them.

Everybody's heart was warmed when the boys did that. But how would we have felt if they had run to the door shouting, "The candy's here! The candy's here!"

Well, I'm afraid that sometimes we do that kind of thing to God. Do we really love God? Or do we just want to get goodies from Him?

God wants us to love Him for who He is, and not just for what He does for us. This is the issue in the Book of Job.

Job was a wealthy man, with a large family. He was a great man in his day. Satan said to God,

> "Doth Job fear God for naught?... But put forth thine hand now, and touch all that he hath, and he will curse thee to thy face." (Job 1:9,11)

But Job remained faithful to God. Then satan said,

> "But put forth thine hand now, and touch his bone and his flesh, and he will curse thee to thy face." (Job 2:5)

But no matter what happened to him, Job did not "sin with his lips." (Job 2:10)

Job's wife told him to "curse God, and die." (Job 2:9) But Job replied,

> "Thou speakest as one of the foolish women speaketh. What? shall we receive good at the hand of God, and shall we not receive evil?" (Job 2:10)

Job complained to God, he demanded explanations, and he showed anger at God. But but he never turned away from God. At the end, when God gave him no explanations, he was content with the fact that he saw God with his own eyes. (Job 42:5) He remained faithful to God for who God was, even though God had allowed satan to take away his family and wealth, and to give him a painful disease. Job served God for who He was and not for what He had given Job.

King David was a worshipper who understood many things about God and His ways. David said,

> "Delight thyself also in the LORD: and he shall give thee the desires of thine heart. Commit thy way unto the LORD; trust also in him; and he shall bring it to pass." (Psalm 37:4-5)

Often, before God is ready to give us the desires of our heart, he may test us to see whether we have truly committed our ways to him and are willing to trust him. It is when things are going "badly" that we have to trust in God because we have nowhere else to turn. Just as He did with Job, God may test us with troubles so that He (and we) can find out whether we are really committed to Him. Do we really love Him and trust Him?

When the three young Hebrews refused to worship Nebuchadnezzar's statue, he threatened to throw them into a very hot furnace. They replied,

> "If it be so, our God whom we serve is able to deliver us from the burning fiery furnace, and he will deliver us out of thine hand, O king. But if not, be it known unto thee, O king, that we will not serve thy gods, nor worship the golden image which thou hast set up." (Daniel 3:17-18)

They believed that God would save them from suffering. But even if He did not, they would serve Him. Their serving God did not depend on what He did or did not do for them, but on who He is.

If God always blessed us with good things, and rescued us from suffering, then we would be tempted to love and serve Him just for what He does for us. Our faith in Him would be based on greed and self-advantage.

God does not want that kind of faith. He wants us to believe in Him, and to love and serve Him, for who He is, and not just for what He does for us. The Apostle Paul demonstrated this when he said,

> "...I know **whom** I have believed, and am persuaded that he is able to keep that which I have committed unto him against that day." (2 Timothy 1:12, emphasis added)

There are many reasons for loving God for who He is. These include His character and His greatness.

God's Character

The important thing to remember about God's character is that it has many aspects. God is loving, compassionate, merciful, forgiving, and kind. He is amazingly patient with us. He also disciplines those he loves. He is holy, righteous, and just. He cannot tolerate evil. He is a God of judgment.

God has all wisdom and all knowledge. He is faithfu. He keeps his promises. He reaches out to us and desires our companionship. He wants us to know him personally. But He is also a great and powerful God. He is awesome in the original and true meaning of that word.

We need to deal with every aspect of God's character. One of the great sources of error in our thinking about God is that we sometimes put so much emphasis on certain aspects of his character that we neglect the others and arrive at a distorted picture. We need to know and follow the whole teaching of Scripture about God, and not just parts of it. For example, Paul wrote,

> "Behold therefore the goodness and severity of God" (Romans 11:22)

This has two aspects to it. First, God is a loving God. God is merciful and patient with us. The Lord longs to be gracious to us. (Isaiah 30:18) He lavishes his grace (his unmerited favor) on those who love him.

"God is love" (1 John 4:16)

"For God so loved the world, that he gave his only begotten Son, that whosoever believeth in him should not perish, but have everlasting life" (John 3:16)

But secondly, God is also just and holy. God will not forever tolerate evil and sin. He is a God of judgment.

"…we shall all stand before the judgment seat of Christ" (Romans 14:10)

Scripture tells us to love God, and also to fear God. How can we do both? How can we both love God and fear Him? This kind of thing happens in normal human life. For example, a young child loves his daddy. But he also fears him, especially when his daddy finds it necessary to discipline him physically.

We need always to be aware of these two aspects of God.

In the past, there were some preachers who put so much emphasis on God's severity that we tended to lose sight of His love and mercy. Today there are many preachers who put such emphasis on God's love and mercy that we tend to lose sight of His wrath and judgment.

Both views are incomplete. Either view, without the other, is a distortion of God's character.

The Greatness of God

God has all wisdom and all knowledge. He is faithful. He keeps his promises. He keeps on reaching out to us. He desires our companionship. He wants us to know him personally. But he is also a great and powerful God.

> "O LORD my God, thou are very great; thou are clothed with honour and majesty" (Psalm 104:1)

> "For the LORD is a great God, and a great King above all gods. In his hand are the deep places of the earth: the strength of the hills is his also. The sea is his, and he made it: and his hands formed the dry land. O come, let us worship and bow down: let us kneel before the Lord our maker. For he is our God; and we are the people of his pasture, and the sheep of his hand." (Psalm 95:3-7)

> "Great is the LORD, and greatly to be praised; and his greatness is unsearchable." (Psalm 145:3)

> "Behold, God is mighty… he is mighty in strength and wisdom." (Job 36:5)

To get some sense of God's greatness, I suggest reading Isaiah, chapter 40, and Revelation, chapters 4 and 5. Even they do not give the whole picture.

God created the earth, the sun, the moon, our solar system, and millions upon millions of stars, most of which are larger than our sun. He created a physical universe that extends (so our scientists tell us) for a huge number of light years. These are distances that most of us cannot begin to grasp. And God is much greater than His creation!

We cannot begin to conceive the full measure of God's greatness, His splendor, His majesty, His power. He has given us, in the Bible, some remarkable visions of Himself. However, they are incomplete and partial. God lives "in unapproachable light, whom no man has seen or can see." (1 Timothy 6:16)

Part of God's greatness is that He is all-powerful. God is the Almighty. That is His nature. That is what it is to be God. God's power is incomparably great. (Ephesians 1:19) He can do all things.

"For with God nothing shall be impossible." (Luke 1:37)

"Is any thing too hard for the LORD? At the time appointed I will return unto thee, according to the time of life, and Sarah shall have a son." (Genesis 18:14)

"I know that thou canst do every thing, and that no thought can be withholden from thee." (Job 42:2)

"But Jesus beheld them, and said unto them, With men this is impossible; but with God all things are possible." (Matthew 19:26)

God's purpose and plans will prevail. Nothing can thwart or defeat them.

"The counsel of the LORD standeth for ever, the thoughts of his heart to all generations." (Psalm 33:11)

"The LORD of hosts hath sworn, saying, Surely as I have thought, so shall it come to pass; and as I have purposed, so shall it stand" (Isaiah 14:24)

The Fear of the Lord

Because God is so great, we should fear Him.

"The fear of the LORD is the beginning of wisdom" (Psalm 111:10)

"The fear of the LORD is clean, enduring forever: the judgments of the LORD are true and righteous altogether." (Psalm 19:9)

"O fear the LORD, ye his saints: for there is no want to them that fear him." (Psalm 34:9)

"The fear of the LORD is the beginning of knowledge" (Proverbs 1:7)

What does it mean, to fear God? I think it means that we recognize God's tremendous power, and His potential for wrath against things that are ungodly. God is not mocked. We need constantly to keep watch over how we live.

It means that we do not presume on God. "Keep back thy servant also from presumptuous sins… and I shall be innocent from the great transgression." (Psalm 19:13)

What are presumptuous sins? We presume on God when we take Him for granted, or seek to manipulate Him. We presume on God when we put Him to the test. (See Matthew 4:7.) Jesus would have presumed on God if He had thrown Himself down from the Temple when God did not tell Him to do so. (See Matthew 4:6-7.)

We presume on God whenever we think we can obligate Him to give us something or to do something on our behalf. God does not owe anything to anybody. He is not obligated to anybody. (See Romans 11:35.)

God is not a heavenly vending machine in which you put in a prayer and get whatever you have asked for. God is sovereign. And note that the Psalmist refers to presumptuous sins as "great transgression."

It means that we recognize that we cannot hide anything from God. God knows us completely. (Psalm 139:1-6) He knows our every thought and action. And we cannot escape from Him.

(Psalm 139:7-12) Even atheists who deny the existence of God will ultimately have to deal with Him.

It means that we are serious about our faith. God wants a total commitment of our lives to Him.

It means that we take the Bible seriously. We don't just ignore Scripture, or give it lip service, or construe it in a way that waters down its clear meaning. It means that we live by what the Bible says, on a daily and hourly basis.

Some people do not like to consider God's greatness because it makes them feel small. That is where God wants us. Scripture tells us to humble ourselves before God. (1 Peter 5:6; James 4:10) This is part of the fear of God, that we recognize how much greater He is than we are.

"...God resisteth the proud, but giveth grace unto the humble." (James 4:6)

Confidence in God

God's greatness also means that, by His incomparably great power working within us, we can conquer whatever problems and difficulties we may have to face. God is bigger. He is bigger than anything we have to deal with.

Nothing is impossible for Him. In Him we can overcome trials and difficulties. It is wonderful to be able to trust in such a great God.

Freedom From Fear

To put it another way, if we fear God, we do not need to fear anything else. If we do not fear God, then we will fear everything else.

Do We Love Him?

In the movie "Fiddler on the Roof," Reb Tevye keeps asking his wife Golde, "Do you love me?" She replies by telling him about all of the things that she has done for him. But Reb Tevye responds by saying, "Yes, but do you love me?"

God has been asking us humans that same question ever since He created Adam and Eve. Do we love Him?

Chapter 17

Don't Give The Devil A Beachhead

"Neither give place to the devil."
(Ephesians 4:27)

Not giving "place" to the devil means that we shouldn't give the devil a beachhead from which he can launch an attack against us. That would also enable the devil to use us to try to harm other people, or to influence them in bad ways. We see an example of that when Jesus told Peter, "Get thee behind me, Satan." (Matthew 16:23)

The Bible talks about the dangers of long-term anger. Now there is such a thing as righteous anger. We see it when Jesus drove the money changers out of the Temple. (John 2:13-17)

Jesus became angry about a bad situation and He did something to make it right. However, He was not an angry man. He was a man who was known primarily for His love and compassion. The Bible warns us not to associate with angry men (or women):

> "Make no friendship with an angry man; and with a furious man thou shalt not go" (Proverbs 22:24)

The point is this. Is anger an identifying mark of our character? Or is it something that shows up occasionally, and appropriately, and then departs quickly? God gave us the emotion of anger for a reason. There are times when it is needed.

Here is an example from my life. Many years ago, I was a live-in housemother in a home for mentally retarded adults. A young man came to visit. (He had been in the same institution that the people in our group home came from.) Within ten minutes, he had all of our people so upset that they were verbally attacking one another. He was a catalyst for discord and confusion and strife. He finally left, and after a while, our people calmed down again.

I made some inquiries and learned that this young man had a reputation for being a trouble maker. And he was dangerous. He had put some counselors in the hospital.

A few weeks later, he showed up again. When I saw him coming up the sidewalk, I turned into a momma bear who was defending her cubs. I was so angry that I didn't care if he put me in the hospital. That boy was NOT going to get into our home again. I confronted him, and he left without hurting me. And he never came back.

I was so angry at that young man that I was willing to risk being injured by him, even to the point of having to be hospitalized. However, I didn't remain angry. Once he was gone, I forgot about him and went back to being a loving housemother.

When anger remains with us, that is when it becomes spiritually dangerous. It can lead us to do sinful things. It can also give the devil a beachhead from which he can attack us (tempt us, confuse us, influence us, etc.):

"Be ye angry, and sin not: let not the sun go down upon your wrath: Neither give place to the devil." (Ephesians 4:26-27)

If we remain angry, then we are in danger of becoming bitter, and according to the Bible, bitterness defiles us. In addition, it is contagious. Our bitterness can cause others to become defiled:

"Follow peace with all men, and holiness, without which no man shall see the Lord: Looking diligently lest any man fail of the grace of God; lest any root of bitterness springing up trouble you, and thereby many be defiled" (Hebrews 12:14-15)

Anger is a strong emotion that can take over and cause us to do harmful things. This is the opposite of being "sober" and "vigilant." Think about people who are drunk. They get carried away by their emotions, and it is easy for them to lose the ability to be alert. Sometimes this can cause practical problems (for example, when they are driving). We cannot afford to be in that state of mind, because we have an enemy who is looking for opportunities to harm us:

"Be sober, be vigilant; because your adversary the devil, as a roaring lion, walketh about, seeking whom he may devour" (1 Peter 5:8)

The Bible tells us that God is "slow to anger," and He wants us to be the same way. Getting angry quickly and easily causes problems. In contrast, being "slow to anger" is a virtue:

"The Lord is gracious, and full of compassion; slow to anger, and of great mercy." (Psalm 145:8)

"He that is slow to anger is better than the mighty; and he that ruleth his spirit than he that taketh a city." (Proverbs 16:32)

"He that is soon angry dealeth foolishly" (Proverbs 14:17)

"Wrath" is stronger than ordinary anger. The Bible warns us to avoid wrath, because it can make us do ungodly things:

"A wrathful man stirreth up strife: but he that is slow to anger appeaseth strife." (Proverbs 15:18)

"Wherefore, my beloved brethren, let every man be swift to hear, slow to speak, **slow to wrath**: For the wrath of man worketh not the righteousness of God." (James 1:19-20, emphasis added)

Wrath can have serious consequences. The Apostle Paul calls it a work of the flesh, and says that it can lead to damnation:

"Now the works of the flesh are manifest, which are these; Adultery, fornication, uncleanness, lasciviousness, Idolatry, witchcraft, hatred, variance [contentions], emulations [jealousy], **wrath**, strife, seditions, heresies, Envyings, murders, drunkenness, revellings, and such like: of the which I tell you before, as I have also told you in time past, that **they which do such things shall not inherit the kingdom of God**." (Galatians 5:19-21, emphasis added)

Notice that Paul lists "wrath" right along with sins like adultery, witchcraft, idolatry, and murder. That makes it very serious. He then contrasts such things with the "fruit of the Spirit":

"But the fruit of the Spirit is love, joy, peace, longsuffering, gentleness, goodness, faith, Meekness, temperance: against such there is no law. And they that are Christ's have crucified the flesh with the affections and lusts." (Galatians 5:22-24)

There is a competition between the "flesh" (our carnal nature) and the Spirit. There is an ongoing struggle between them. Our carnal nature makes it difficult for us to live the way that God wants us to live. We want to do the right thing, but our "flesh" gets in the way:

"This I say then, Walk in the Spirit, and ye shall not fulfil the lust of the flesh. For the flesh lusteth against the Spirit, and the Spirit against the flesh: and these are contrary the one to the other: so that ye cannot do the things that ye would." (Galatians 5:16-17)

There is an old story about a man who told his friend, "I feel like there are two dogs fighting inside of me." His friend asked, "Which one is winning?" And he replied, "The one I feed the most."

We need to feed the Godly side of us, and starve the carnal side. Prayer, worship, Scripture, and the fellowship of solid Christian friends helps feed the Godly side.

There is an expression, "nursing a grudge." According to *Webster's Dictionary*, a grudge is "a feeling of deep-seated resentment or ill will." In other words, it's a form of long-term anger.

Think about what nursing mothers do. They look at their baby, feed him, caress him, and talk to him. They become totally focussed on that baby, and nourish him so that he can grow big and strong.

What does it mean to "nurse a grudge"? To keep feeding it, and thinking about it, and focussing on it. Of course, that makes it keep growing. It gets bigger and stronger.

That is the exact opposite of what we should do as Christians. We should starve that grudge, and do everything that we can to kill it. We cannot afford to have long-term anger. That gives the devil a beachhead, which is spiritually dangerous for us. In addition, when the devil is able to work on us, then we may wind up hurting other people.

Long-term anger can take the form of resentment. Sometimes it can appear to be "righteous indignation." The problem is, if it remains—if it continues—then it stops being righteous.

Long-term anger can also take the form of being offended. If somebody does something offensive, that does not mean that we have to become offended. As Christians, we need to learn to respond Biblically instead of reacting carnally. It's a learning process that requires time, thought, and prayer. It's a skill that we need to develop.

Think about the term "to take offense." Somebody does something hurtful, something to offend you. Well, picture that as being like an object that the person just put on the table in front of you. They put it there. But it is up to you to decide whether or not to "take" it. Are you going to pick it up? Or are you going to leave it there?

We do not have to take offense just because somebody does something offensive to us. We can choose not to take offense. We can choose to leave it alone.

Anger can also take the form of being annoyed, exasperated, frustrated, or indignant. We all have times of feeling that way. As long as it is only temporary, and we don't do anything sinful as a result of it, that's alright. However, if it continues—if it becomes long-term—then we have a problem.

> "Be ye angry, and sin not: let not the sun go down upon your wrath: Neither give place to the devil." (Ephesians 4:26-27)

When we are angry, it is easy for us to say and do things that hurt other people. If the ones we hurt are Christians, then God counts it as having done those things to Jesus Christ.

We see this when Jesus appeared to Saul when he was on the road to Damascus. (Paul was called Saul before he became a Christian.) Paul had been actively persecuting Christians, but Jesus said that Paul had been persecuting **Him** (Jesus). We also see it when Jesus told us about how God will separate the sheep from the goats:

> "And he fell to the earth, and heard a voice saying unto him, Saul, Saul, why persecutest thou **me**? And he said, Who art thou, Lord? And the Lord said, **I am Jesus**

whom thou persecutest: it is hard for thee to kick against the pricks." (Acts 9:4-5, emphasis added)

"When the Son of man shall come in his glory, and all the holy angels with him, then shall he sit upon the throne of his glory: And before him shall be gathered all nations: and he shall separate them one from another, as a shepherd divideth his sheep from the goats: And he shall set the sheep on his right hand, but the goats on the left. Then shall the King say unto them on his right hand, Come, ye blessed of my Father, inherit the kingdom prepared for you from the foundation of the world: For I was an hungred, and ye gave me meat: I was thirsty, and ye gave me drink: I was a stranger, and ye took me in: Naked, and ye clothed me: I was sick, and ye visited me: I was in prison, and ye came unto me. Then shall the righteous answer him, saying, Lord, when saw we thee an hungred, and fed thee? or thirsty, and gave thee drink? When saw we thee a stranger, and took thee in? or naked, and clothed thee? Or when saw we thee sick, or in prison, and came unto thee? And the King shall answer and say unto them, Verily I say unto you, **Inasmuch as ye have done it unto one of the least of these my brethren, ye have done it unto me.**" (Matthew 25:31-40, emphasis added)

One form that long-term anger can take is self-condemnation. For some people, this is a real problem. We sinned. We repented. God forgave us. He took our sins away from us. The Bible says:

"He hath not dealt with us after our sins; nor rewarded us according to our iniquities. For as the heaven is high above the earth, so great is his mercy toward them that fear him. **As far as the east is from the west, so far hath he removed our transgressions from us**. Like as a father pitieth his children, so the Lord pitieth them that fear him." (Psalm 103:10-13, emphasis added)

East and west never meet. No matter how far you travel east, you never wind up going west. That is very different from north and south, which meet at the North Pole and the South Pole.

God goes even further than that. Once we repent and He forgives us, then He doesn't even remember our sins. He told us:

" I, even I, am he that blotteth out thy transgressions for mine own sake, and will not remember thy sins." (Isaiah 43:25)

Now if God has put away our sins, and He doesn't remember them any more, then who are we to keep dredging them up and beating ourselves up about them? This can actually be a form of pride. It is saying that our standards are higher than God's standards are.

Remember that Jesus said, "Inasmuch as ye have done it unto one of the least of these my brethren, ye have done it unto me." (Matthew 25:40) Because we are Christians, that applies to us as much as to other people. When we keep beating ourselves over the heads for sins that God has already forgiven, then we are tormenting one of God's people (namely ourselves). God counts that as doing it to Jesus.

The Apostle Paul must have struggled with that problem. Before he became a Christian, he rounded up Christians and had them put to death. He must have encountered many Christians who knew people, or were related to people, that Paul was responsible for killing. Paul said:

"Brethren, I count not myself to have apprehended: but this one thing I do, **forgetting those things which are behind**, and reaching forth unto those things which are before, I press toward the mark for the prize of the high calling of God in Christ Jesus." (Philippians 3:13-14, emphasis added)

One of the things that Paul had to put behind him, and not look back at, was his past sin of persecuting Christians.

We need to forgive everybody. That includes ourselves.

In the Book of Revelation, the devil is called "the accuser of the brethren." (Revelation 12:10) Why should we do the devil's job for him?

We need to forgive others, instead of accusing them. And once we have repented of our sins, then we need to stop accusing ourselves.

The conviction of the Holy Spirit draws us closer to God. It gets us to focus on Him, and repent of our sins. In contrast, self condemnation gets us to focus on ourselves instead of God.

When you drive down a country road, there are ditches on both sides of the road. If you go too far to the right, you will wind up in one ditch, and if you go too far to the left, you will wind up in the opposite ditch.

When it comes to our sins, there are two ditches that we can fall into. One ditch is to ignore our sins, or deny them, or not take them seriously. The other ditch is to keep hitting ourselves over the heads because of them, long after we have repented of them and God has forgotten them. We need to avoid both ditches.

Some people fall into both ditches at the same time. They have such a serious problem with self condemnation that acknowledging their sins has become unbearable for them. And as a result, they deny their sins.

The answer to that problem is to treat self condemnation as being some of the "fiery darts" that the enemy throws at us. (Ephesians 6:16) We need to consciously refuse to play that game. We need to get our focus off of ourselves and back on to God. We need to develop the discipline of refusing to get into self condemnation.

During times of persecution, this becomes especially important because the world will keep accusing us. And not just for our faults. It will condemn the good things that we say and do. It will call good things evil. God said:

> "Woe unto them that call evil good, and good evil; that put darkness for light, and light for darkness; that put bitter for sweet, and sweet for bitter!" (Isaiah 5:20)

God would not have said that if people didn't do it. And unfortunately, they do. It has become widespread in America. It is being done by the media, by the entertainment industry, and by teachers in public schools and universities.

It is also being done by some psychiatrists. For example, Dr. Brock Chisholm wants to destroy our ability to tell the difference between good and evil. He is the psychiatrist who was the first Secretary-General of the United Nations' World Health Organization, so he is in a position of great power and influence. He is one of the people that Psalm 2 talks about:

> "The kings of the earth set themselves, and the rulers take counsel together, against the LORD, and against his anointed" (Psalm 2:2)

Dr. Chisholm and the other ungodly "movers and shakers" who have an anti-Christian agenda have no idea of what is at stake for them. It does not pay to mess with God. Unless they wake up and repent, they will come to a bad end:

> "Thou shalt break them with a rod of iron; thou shalt dash them in pieces like a potter's vessel." (Psalm 2:9)

When I was a girl, the only evil people I knew about were the ones I read about in books. I also saw bad guys in cowboy movies on TV. Those were people from other countries, or other times.

They were not in my real world. Unfortunately, things have changed. Today, I often read about evil people in the news, and sometimes I run into them in person.

If persecution increases, then we may see terrible things done by wicked people. If that happens, then we will have to be on guard against long-term anger. Of course, anger will rise up in us from time to time, but we cannot afford to let it remain.

There is an old saying that "You can't keep a bird from flying overhead, but you can keep it from building a nest in your hair." The same is true of anger. We can't help getting angry at times, but we don't have to stay angry.

One good antidote to anger is to remember that God is going to take care of the bad guys. They will pay for what they are doing—unless they repent and get saved, which would be much better. Jesus died to save them. He paid a terrible price in order to enable them to be saved, and He should get what he paid for. So we should pray for their salvation.

It is always wonderful to hear testimonies of terrorists and hit men and drug dealers and nasty bikers who become Christians. I love it when really bad guys get saved. That demonstrates what a mighty God we serve. Once they become Christians, such people are as zealous and bold for God as they used to be for doing bad things.

However, if they do not get saved, then God will deal with them. So for us, it's a win/win situation. If they get saved, then we will have a new brother or sister in Christ, and we can be reconciled. And if they don't, then God will punish them for the evil that they have done to us and to others. They will pay a heavy price for it.

In the following Scripture quotation, the term "give place unto wrath" means leaving room for God's wrath, as opposed to ours. God can have wrath that is absolutely righteous, because He is holy. But we are sinful people, even though we have been saved by grace. Therefore, when we get angry (especially if it gets to the point of "wrath"), it is easy for us to fall into sin. So it is better (and spiritually much safer) to leave the wrath to God:

> "Dearly beloved, avenge not yourselves, but rather give place unto wrath: for it is written, Vengeance is mine; I will repay, saith the Lord." (Romans 12:19)

There are many places in the Bible that talk about how God deals with wicked men and those who do evil things. Here are a few of them:

> "The ungodly are not so: but are like the chaff which the wind driveth away. Therefore the ungodly shall not stand in the judgment, nor sinners in the congregation of the righteous. For the Lord knoweth the way of the righteous: but the way of the ungodly shall perish." (Psalm 1:4-6)

> "Thou hast rebuked the heathen, thou hast destroyed the wicked, thou hast put out their name for ever and ever." (Psalm 9:5)

> "Surely thou didst set them in slippery places: thou castedst them down into destruction. How are they brought into desolation, as in a moment! they are utterly consumed with terrors." (Psalm 73:18-19)

> "Thou shalt break them with a rod of iron; thou shalt dash them in pieces like a potter's vessel." (Psalm 2:9)

> "Wait on the Lord, and keep his way, and he shall exalt thee to inherit the land: when the wicked are cut off, thou shalt see it. I have seen the wicked in great power, and spreading himself like a green bay tree. Yet he passed away, and, lo, he was not: yea, I sought him, but he could not be found." (Psalm 37:34-36)

"Rest in the Lord, and wait patiently for him: fret not thyself because of him who prospereth in his way, because of the man who bringeth wicked devices to pass. Cease from anger, and forsake wrath: fret not thyself in any wise to do evil. For evildoers shall be cut off: but those that wait upon the Lord, they shall inherit the earth. For yet a little while, and the wicked shall not be: yea, thou shalt diligently consider his place, and it shall not be. But the meek shall inherit the earth; and shall delight themselves in the abundance of peace." (Psalm 37:7-11)

According to *Webster's Dictionary*, the word "meek" means "enduring injury with patience and without resentment." It can also mean "submissive," but the primary meaning is what the Bible calls being "longsuffering." I have seen it defined as being "strength under control."[1] To put it in terms of animals, "meek" does not mean being a helpless mouse. It means being a patient lion.

A good antidote to anger is to major on learning to love, as love is described in the Bible. (Sometimes the Bible refers to love as "charity.") Love should be the hallmark of a Christian:

"By this shall all men know that ye are my disciples, if ye have love one to another." (John 13:35)

"Charity suffereth long, and is kind; charity envieth not; charity vaunteth not itself, is not puffed up, Doth not behave itself unseemly, seeketh not her own, **is not easily provoked**, thinketh no evil; Rejoiceth not in iniquity, but rejoiceth in the truth; Beareth all things, believeth all things, hopeth all things, endureth all things." (1 Corinthians 13:4-7, emphasis added)

"Put on therefore, as the elect of God, holy and beloved, bowels of **mercies**, kindness, humbleness of mind, meekness, **longsuffering**; Forbearing one another, and **forgiving one another**, if any man have a quarrel against any: even **as Christ forgave you, so also do ye**. And above all these things put on charity, which is the bond of perfectness. And let the peace of God rule in your hearts, to the which also ye are called in one body; and be ye thankful." (Colossians 3:12-15, emphasis added)

God is our Father. We are just children compared to Him. We need to leave the "heavy lifting" to Him, because He can handle it and we can't. That includes letting Him take care of the bad guys.

When there are practical things that we can do to protect ourselves and those we love, then we should do it. Also, there are times when evildoers can be brought to justice. In that case, we should help do that if we are in a position to do so.

When it comes to serious persecution, there isn't much that we can do about the bad guys. Jews who survived the Holocaust know that. So do the Middle Eastern Christians who live in nations where Christians are being beheaded and burned alive. In extreme situations like that, all that we can do is endure the hardship and trust the Lord:

"Thou therefore endure hardness, as a good soldier of Jesus Christ." (2 Timothy 2:3)

"He shall not be afraid of evil tidings: his heart is fixed, trusting in the Lord." (Psalm 112:7)

Could something like that happen here in America? It's possible. No nation is immune to such things if it turns away from God. Unfortunately, there are many parallels between modern America and Germany in the days before Hitler became a full-fledged dictator.

Thankfully, we are never at the mercy of men or of circumstances, because God is able to make **all** things work out for our long-term, eternal good if we love Him. There are no exceptions. He can use bad situations to bring us closer to Him, to teach us to love Him and trust Him more, and to bear good fruit in our lives which we will enjoy for all eternity:

> "And we know that all things work together for good to them that love God, to them who are the called according to his purpose." (Romans 8:28)

> "Who shall separate us from the love of Christ? shall tribulation, or distress, or persecution, or famine, or nakedness, or peril, or sword? As it is written, For thy sake we are killed all the day long; we are accounted as sheep for the slaughter. Nay, in all these things **we are more than conquerors through him that loved us**." (Romans 8:35-37, emphasis added)

We will go through some difficult things. At times we won't understand why these things are happening or how it is possible for them to happen. That is when it is good to remind ourselves that only God sees the really big picture. Our understanding is valuable, but it is limited:

> "Trust in the Lord with all thine heart; and lean not unto thine own understanding. In all thy ways acknowledge him, and he shall direct thy paths." (Proverbs 3:5-6)

Paul described our life as Christians as being like people who are running in a race—and runners have to look forward. If they look back while they are running, then they will slow down, and they are in danger of running into someone or tripping over something. They have to keep looking foreword:

> "Wherefore seeing we also are compassed about with so great a cloud of witnesses, let us lay aside every weight,

and the sin which doth so easily beset us, and let us **run with patience the race that is set before us**, Looking unto Jesus the author and finisher of our faith; who for the joy that was set before him endured the cross, despising the shame, and is set down at the right hand of the throne of God." (Hebrews 12:1-2, emphasis added)

"Brethren, I count not myself to have apprehended: but this one thing I do, **forgetting those things which are behind**, and **reaching forth unto those things which are before**, I press toward the mark for the prize of the high calling of God in Christ Jesus." (Philippians 3:13-14, emphasis added)

Of course, it is always good to remember the many ways that God has been faithful to us, and the mercy that He has shown us, and the truth that He has taught us. But when it comes to hurtful things that people did to us, we need to forgive the people, and move on, and leave the hurts behind us.

LEAVING THE PAST BEHIND
(by Maria Kneas)

Following Jesus, my Lord and my Savior,
Leaving the past behind.

I press on to the mark of God's high calling,
Leaving the past behind.

Forgiving, forgetting, and giving to Jesus,
Leaving the past behind.

Chapter 18

Giving Thanks To God

"In every thing give thanks: for this is the will of God in Christ Jesus concerning you." (1 Thessalonians 5:18)

I heard about an old woman with painful arthritis who struggled to climb a hill. When she got to the top, she looked at the view and said, "God, why did You make the world so beautiful?"

I'm afraid that many of us would have been complaining about the pain and the difficulty in walking, instead of giving thanks for the beauty. I've been guilty of doing that kind of thing myself.

When we are suffering, it is so easy to tell God, "It's not fair! Why did You let this happen to me?" But how often do we turn to God and say, "Why did You save me? I deserved to go to hell. Why do You love me when I have been so unfaithful to you? Why are You so patient with me when I become stubborn and rebellious?"

It's so easy to take good things for granted and to focus on our problems. Our default setting seems to be self-pity and a sense of entitlement.

The Bible has a lot to say about the importance of praise and thanksgiving. Here are a few examples:

"Rejoice in the Lord always: and again I say, Rejoice. Let your moderation be known unto all men. The Lord is at hand. Be careful [anxious] for nothing; but in every thing by prayer and supplication with thanksgiving let your requests be made known unto God. And the peace of God, which passeth all understanding, shall keep your hearts and minds through Christ Jesus." (Philippians 4:4-7)

"I will bless the Lord at all times: his praise shall continually be in my mouth. My soul shall make her boast in the Lord: the humble shall hear thereof, and be glad. O magnify the Lord with me, and let us exalt his name together." (Psalm 34:1-3)

"Rejoice evermore. Pray without ceasing. In every thing give thanks: for this is the will of God in Christ Jesus concerning you." (1 Thessalonians 5:16-18)

"O Lord, open thou my lips; and my mouth shall shew forth thy praise." (Psalm 51:15)

God created us and gave us a beautiful world to live in. After Adam and Eve fell into sin, Jesus died on the cross to save us. And God has Heaven waiting for us. Compared to those blessings, anything that we suffer now is small and temporary. The Apostle Paul said:

"For our light affliction, which is but for a moment, worketh for us a far more exceeding and eternal weight of glory" (2 Corinthians 4:17)

Here are some of the things that Paul called a "light" affliction. I would not want to have to go through any of them, but Christians in countries with severe persecution suffer many similar things. Therefore, we need to be prepared to endure such things if necessary. We also need to have Paul's perspective about them. That is Biblical, and it is based on reality—on the nature and character of God, and the importance of Eternity.

Here are some of the things that Paul went through. We know that he also went through other traumatic things. The Book of

Acts tells us about times when he was attacked by angry mobs. At one point, Paul went through something that was so severe that he "despaired even of life." (2 Corinthians 1:8) Here is what Paul said:

> "Of the Jews five times received I forty stripes save one. Thrice was I beaten with rods, once was I stoned, thrice I suffered shipwreck, a night and a day I have been in the deep; In journeyings often, in perils of waters, in perils of robbers, in perils by mine own countrymen, in perils by the heathen, in perils in the city, in perils in the wilderness, in perils in the sea, in perils among false brethren; In weariness and painfulness, in watchings often, in hunger and thirst, in fastings often, in cold and nakedness." (2 Corinthians 11:24-27)

Lack of gratitude to God can result in serious consequences. In the first chapter of Paul's Epistle to the Romans, we see a horrible downhill spiral. It's a slippery slope that escalates into depravity and destruction. Notice that the starting point is a lack of gratitude and respect for God. In the beginning, they knew God, but they refused to give Him glory, and they were not thankful.

It gets to the point where they "did not like to retain God in their knowledge." In other words, they used to know that God is real. Deep down inside, they still know it. In spite of that, they deny God's existence. They try to find reasons for not believing in Him.

That would explain why we see militant atheists who hate God. How can you hate somebody who doesn't exist? At some level, they know better. Otherwise, they would not be able to hate Him. There are even some atheists who say that they want to "kill the God of Christianity." [1]

Here is the Apostle Paul's description of this deadly downhill slide:

"Because that, **when they knew God, they glorified him not as God, neither were thankful**; but became vain in their imaginations, and their foolish heart was darkened. Professing themselves to be wise, they became fools, And changed the glory of the uncorruptible God into an image made like to corruptible man, and to birds, and fourfooted beasts, and creeping things. Wherefore God also gave them up to uncleanness through the lusts of their own hearts, to dishonour their own bodies between themselves: Who changed the truth of God into a lie, and worshipped and served the creature more than the Creator, who is blessed for ever. Amen. For this cause God gave them up unto vile affections: for even their women did change the natural use into that which is against nature: And likewise also the men, leaving the natural use of the woman, burned in their lust one toward another; men with men working that which is unseemly, and receiving in themselves that recompence of their error which was meet. And even as **they did not like to retain God in their knowledge**, God gave them over to a reprobate mind, to do those things which are not convenient; Being filled with all unrighteousness, fornication, wickedness, covetousness, maliciousness; full of envy, murder, debate, deceit, malignity; whisperers, Backbiters, haters of God, despiteful, proud, boasters, **inventors of evil things**, disobedient to parents, Without understanding, covenant-breakers, without natural affection, implacable, unmerciful: Who knowing the judgment of God, that they which commit such things are worthy of death, not only do the same, but have pleasure in them that do them." (Romans 1:21-32, emphasis added)

Unfortunately, this is a good description of where much of America is at today. We see many people in various stages of this downhill slide. The media and the entertainment industry actively promote it. So do our public schools.

The antidote is to have a grateful heart and to give thanks to God. This does not come naturally. We have to develop the habit of giving thanks.

Have you ever noticed that people who complain keep finding more and more things to complain about? In contrast, people who are thankful keep finding more and more reasons to give thanks.

We have a choice to make. Either we can become more and more grateful to God, or else we can become more and more full of complaining and self-pity. Eventually, that can end in becoming bitter. The Bible warns us that bitterness is both deadly and contagious:

> "Follow peace with all men, and holiness, without which no man shall see the Lord: Looking diligently lest any man fail of the grace of God; lest any root of bitterness springing up trouble you, and thereby many be defiled" (Hebrews 12:14-15)

Praising God and giving thanks to Him increases our faith. It also makes us more aware of God's presence, His love, His power, and His faithfulness. Lack of praise and gratitude hinders our relationship with God. That makes us more vulnerable to doubts and temptations.

To put it in medical terms, you could say that praise and thanksgiving strengthen our spiritual immune system. It protects us both spiritually and emotionally. It helps us grow stronger and have more energy and focus to live Biblically and do whatever God has called us to do.

Praising God and showing gratitude to Him can take many forms. One is singing hymns and worship songs. The Bible strongly encourages us to do that:

"Speaking to yourselves in psalms and hymns and spiritual songs, singing and making melody in your heart to the Lord; Giving thanks always for all things unto God and the Father in the name of our Lord Jesus Christ" (Ephesians 5:19-20)

This means more than singing in church. It means singing when we are driving, or washing the dishes, or taking a shower. And it means singing "in our hearts" (silently) in addition to singing out loud.

I have a friend who memorizes a lot of Scripture, and he praises the Lord by quoting Scripture or talking to God in Biblical terms. He uses Scripture passages that are appropriate for the situation that he is in at the moment.

I knew a mentally retarded lady named Nancy whose mental age was about two years old. She loved God so much. If she saw a Bible, she would pick it up and stroke it and hold it against her heart. She was unable to read, but she knew that the Bible was God's Word, and she loved it. One day somebody gave her a painting of Jesus. She kissed it and started dancing. Nancy was very limited in her ability to express herself verbally, so she showed her joy and love and gratitude by dancing.

Eric Lidell said that when he ran, he could feel God's pleasure. He ran in order to glorify God, and to please God. After he won the Olympics, Eric became a missionary. His fame as an athlete gave him a platform for telling people about Jesus. They came to see the famous runner, but they wound up learning about God.

There is another way to praise and glorify God. Because persecution is increasing, many of us will be called to do it. Jesus said:

"Whosoever therefore shall confess me before men, him will I confess also before my Father which is in heaven. But whosoever shall deny me before men, him will I also deny before my Father which is in heaven." (Matthew 10:32-33)

This can take many forms. The most extreme is when Christians in the Middle East are told to renounce their faith or be killed. In America, right now it is more likely to be the challenge to either acknowledge or else deny Biblical truths and Biblical morality. For example, a Christian baker in America refused to bake a wedding cake for a homosexual wedding. The judge told the baker that this violates the antidiscrimination law of Colorado, and unless he bakes cakes for homosexual weddings, he will be fined and he may even be sent to prison.

Another way to glorify God is to die for Him. Some people are called to be martyrs. Jesus made it clear that it was God's will for Peter to be martyred:

"Verily, verily, I say unto thee, When thou wast young, thou girdest thyself, and walkedst whither thou wouldest: but when thou shalt be old, thou shalt stretch forth thy hands, and another shall gird thee, and carry thee whither thou wouldest not. This spake he, **signifying by what death he should glorify God**. And when he had spoken this, he saith unto him, Follow me." (John 21:18-19, emphasis added)

God told us to protect ourselves and our families from persecution, if we can do so without denying Him. However, we need to be willing to die for Him if necessary. We need to love God more than we love our lives:

"But when they persecute you in this city, flee ye into another" (Matthew 10:23)

"Precious in the sight of the Lord is the death of his saints." (Psalm 116:15)

"And they overcame him by the blood of the Lamb, and by the word of their testimony; and they loved not their lives unto the death." (Revelation 12:11)

LIGHT AFTER DARKNESS
(by Frances Ridley Havergal, 1879)

Light after darkness, gain after loss,
Strength after suffering, crown after cross.
Sweet after bitter, song after sigh,
Home after wandering, praise after cry.

Sheaves after sowing, sun after rain,
Sight after mystery, peace after pain.
Joy after sorrow, calm after blast,
Rest after weariness, sweet rest at last.

Near after distant, gleam after gloom,
Love after loneliness, life after tomb.
After long agony, rapture of bliss!
Right was the pathway leading to this!

(Public domain)

Chapter 19

Jesus Told Us To Forgive

"And when ye stand praying, forgive, if ye have ought against any: that your Father also which is in heaven may forgive you your trespasses." (Mark 11:25)

Jesus told us to forgive the people who hurt us, and He said it in very strong terms. There are serious consequences if we fail to forgive. When He taught the disciples the Lord's Prayer, Jesus said:

"And forgive us our debts, **as we forgive** our debtors." (Matthew 6:12, emphasis added)

The Bible is very clear about this. If we don't forgive others, then God will not forgive us. Jesus emphasized this even further with the very first statement that He made after teaching them the Lord's Prayer. He said:

"For if ye forgive men their trespasses, your heavenly Father will also forgive you: But **if ye forgive not men their trespasses, neither will your Father forgive your trespasses**." (Matthew 6:14-15, emphasis added)

One of the Beatitudes relates to forgiveness. We need mercy from God. Therefore, we need to be merciful to others. Jesus said:

"Blessed are the merciful: for they shall obtain mercy." (Matthew 5:7)

Do people who do nasty things deserve mercy? Of course not. They deserve hell. But so do we. Every one of us is a sinner, and we all deserve to go to hell. The only reason we can go to Heaven is because Jesus died for our sins. He was loving and merciful and forgiving with us when we did not deserve it at all. On the contrary, we were rebellious sinners who deserved eternal damnation. We need to follow the example of Jesus and show love and mercy to others:

"But God commendeth his love toward us, in that, while we were yet sinners, Christ died for us." (Romans 5:8)

Jesus told us that we will reap what we sow. Therefore, if we sow mercy and forgiveness, then we will reap them. If we sow unforgiveness, then that is what we will reap:

"Be not deceived; God is not mocked: for whatsoever a man soweth, that shall he also reap." (Galatians 6:7)

Have you ever done any farming or gardening? One small seed can result in a large plant. I counted the number of grains on an ear of corn, and there were about 500 of them. If you planted one of those grains, you would get a plant with two or three ears of corn on it. That would be 1,000 to 1,500 times as many grains as you planted. This demonstrates that we need to be careful about what we sow, because we are going to get a lot of it back.

Sometimes it can be very difficult to forgive. In that case, we can ask God to make us willing to do it, and to enable us to do it. He said that His grace is sufficient for us. That includes the grace to do difficult things like forgiving those who have done terrible things to us, or to those we love. We can do whatever we need to do (including forgiving) because Jesus Christ will give us the strength to do it:

Prepare for Persecution

"And he said unto me, My grace is sufficient for thee: for my strength is made perfect in weakness. Most gladly therefore will I rather glory in my infirmities, that the power of Christ may rest upon me." (2 Corinthians 12:9)

"I can do all things through Christ which strengtheneth me." (Philippians 4:13)

Sometimes forgiving is a gradual process that takes time, like working through the layers of an onion. You get through one layer, and think that you have gotten it done. And then you realize that you need to go deeper, and forgive at a deeper level. If we have been seriously hurt, it may take a long time, even years. The important thing is to be moving in the right direction—to forgive as much as we are able to at the moment, and ask God to enable us to do it more completely.

Corrie ten Boom and her sister Betsy were sent to a Nazi concentration camp because they hid Jews in their home. The guards were cruel, and they did some terrible things. Betsy was able to forgive them right away. She saw them as being like trapped, tormented animals, and she prayed for them. But it was different with Corrie. At first, she hated the guards, and she hated all Nazis. She had to keep praying and asking God to make her able to forgive. And finally, after a long struggle, she was able to do it.

Betsy died in that camp, but Corrie survived. After the war, she traveled the world, telling people about God's love and forgiveness. She even ministered to one of the guards, and to a German nurse who had done something cruel to them in that camp.

On a practical note, forgiving somebody does not mean that we trust them. If a person is harmful or dangerous, then we have to protect ourselves and our loved ones from them.

In some cases, we may not be able to tell the person that we forgive them, because having any contact with them would be dangerous for us. But we can still forgive them, and we can pray for them. We can ask God to soften their hearts and open their eyes and bring them to salvation.

When Jesus sent the twelve apostles out to heal the sick and cast out demons, we have no record that they asked for more faith in order to be able to do it. They just went out and did it. However, when Jesus told them that they had to keep on forgiving, that is when they asked Him to increase their faith. They already had enough faith to do miracles, but forgiving was more difficult:

> "Take heed to yourselves: If thy brother trespass against thee, rebuke him; and if he repent, forgive him. And if he trespass against thee seven times in a day, and seven times in a day turn again to thee, saying, I repent; thou shalt forgive him. And the apostles said unto the Lord, Increase our faith." (Luke 17:3-5)

Jesus told a very sobering parable about the importance of being merciful and forgiving. It talks about a servant who owed his master 10,000 talents. According to my study Bible, that is "an incomprehensible amount of money." The parable also talks about another servant who owed money to the servant who had the huge debt. He owed 100 denarii, which is about three months' wages. That's a lot of money, but compared to 10,000 talents, it isn't much. Here is the parable:

> "Therefore is the kingdom of heaven likened unto a certain king, which would take account of his servants. And when he had begun to reckon, one was brought unto him, which owed him ten thousand talents. But forasmuch as he had not to pay, his lord commanded him to be sold, and his wife, and children, and all that he had, and payment to be made. The servant therefore fell down, and worshipped him, saying, Lord, have patience with me, and

I will pay thee all. Then the lord of that servant was moved with compassion, and loosed him, and forgave him the debt. But the same servant went out, and found one of his fellowservants, which owed him an hundred pence: and he laid hands on him, and took him by the throat, saying, Pay me that thou owest. And his fellowservant fell down at his feet, and besought him, saying, Have patience with me, and I will pay thee all. And he would not: but went and cast him into prison, till he should pay the debt. So when his fellowservants saw what was done, they were very sorry, and came and told unto their lord all that was done. Then his lord, after that he had called him, said unto him, O thou wicked servant, I forgave thee all that debt, because thou desiredst me: Shouldest not thou also have had compassion on thy fellowservant, even as I had pity on thee? And his lord was wroth, and **delivered him to the tormentors**, till he should pay all that was due unto him. **So likewise shall my heavenly Father do also unto you, if ye from your hearts forgive not every one his brother their trespasses.**" (Matthew 18:23-35, emphasis added)

The wicked servant was turned over to the "tormenters" until he paid the debt. But he would never be able to pay it. That debt was so large that it would be extremely difficult (if not impossible) to pay it back even if the servant had a well paying job. A man who is in prison can't earn much money, which means that there was no way that he could ever pay that debt. So in effect, the wicked servant was sentenced to being tortured for the rest of his life.

Have you ever noticed that bitter people who don't forgive are tormented people? Everything reminds them of their grievance, of the wrong that was done to them and the person (or people) who did it. That grievance becomes the center of their life. They become hard and harsh, and they wind up hurting other people because of their bad attitude.

The wrong that was done to them is not the source of their problem. The thing that causes them to be tormented is the state of their own heart.

There is an old saying that "The same sun that softens wax hardens clay."

We can see an example of that with Corrie and Betsy ten Boom. They suffered greatly in a Nazi concentration camp, and went through many traumatic experiences. But the end result was that they became sweeter and more loving. They helped many women in that camp come closer to God. Christian women were strengthened and encouraged, and some nonbelievers came to salvation. At the same time, I'm sure that there were many other women there who became hard and bitter.

If we have a heart for God, and we are willing to do things His way (which includes forgiving), then there is absolutely nothing that can destroy us. It may cause us temporary suffering, but the end result will be getting closer to God and knowing Him better. In the end, we will be grateful that we went through that experience because of the good fruit that it bore in our lives. That good fruit is something that we will enjoy for all eternity:

> "Nay, in all these things we are more than conquerors through him that loved us." (Romans 8:37)

> "My brethren, count it all joy when ye fall into divers temptations; Knowing this, that the trying of your faith worketh patience. But let patience have her perfect work, that ye may be perfect and entire, wanting nothing." (James 1:2-4)

> "But the fruit of the Spirit is love, joy, peace, longsuffering, gentleness, goodness, faith, Meekness, temperance" (Galatians 5:22-23)

"Blessed are ye, when men shall revile you, and persecute you, and shall say all manner of evil against you falsely, for my sake. **Rejoice, and be exceeding glad: for great is your reward in heaven**: for so persecuted they the prophets which were before you." (Matthew 5:11-12, emphasis added)

"Blessed is the man that endureth temptation: for when he is tried, he shall receive the crown of life, which the Lord hath promised to them that love him." (James 1:12)

"For our light affliction, which is but for a moment, worketh for us a far more exceeding and eternal weight of glory" (2 Corinthians 4:17)

"For I reckon that the sufferings of this present time are not worthy to be compared with the glory which shall be revealed in us." (Romans 8:18)

"For the Lamb which is in the midst of the throne shall feed them, and shall lead them unto living fountains of waters: and God shall wipe away all tears from their eyes." (Revelation 7:17)

"And God shall wipe away all tears from their eyes; and there shall be no more death, neither sorrow, nor crying, neither shall there be any more pain: for the former things are passed away. And he that sat upon the throne said, Behold, I make all things new." (Revelation 21:4-5)

*"I would permit no man
to narrow and degrade my soul
by making me hate him."*

(Booker T. Washington)

Chapter 20

The Importance Of Integrity

Recently I was talking with a friend and she said, "These days, most people have no idea of the importance of integrity." Unfortunately, that is all too true. To show how much things have changed, when it came to business deals, my grandfather's handshake was worth more than a modern legal contract.

As Christians, we cannot afford to compromise our faith or Biblical morality. The world is going to put us under a lot of pressure to do it. Therefore, we need to be determined ahead of time to stand our ground.

In the Navy, the term "integrity" means "water tight." In other words, a ship with no leaks.

We all know about the Titanic. After it hit the iceberg, it sank within a few hours. That collision created a huge leak which was obviously disastrous. However, small leaks can also sink ships. It just takes longer. In addition, as water comes in through the leak, the pressure makes the hole get larger and larger. In other words, the leak incrementally gets bigger.

The world will pressure us to deny God in two ways. One method is by obvious, intense pressure. The other method is incrementally—one small step at a time, which makes it much more difficult to notice. Therefore, we have to be vigilant.

We need to keep our faith and our morality Biblical and not allow them to become compromised. Not even in ways that seem to be small. The stakes are so high that we cannot afford to compromise:

> "For what is a man profited, if he shall gain the whole world, and lose his own soul? or what shall a man give in exchange for his soul?" (Matthew 16:26)

One area that we need to guard is being truthful in our words and in our actions. We need to be men and women of truth. Our post-modern culture has become so permeated with lies and deception that people have become desensitized to it. However, God takes this very seriously:

> "But the fearful, and unbelieving, and the abominable, and murderers, and whoremongers, and sorcerers, and idolaters, and **all liars**, shall have their part in the lake which burneth with fire and brimstone: which is the second death." (Revelation 21:8, emphasis added)

I think that by "fearful" it means people who allow fear to prevent them from following God and living according to His standards. We all feel fear at times. The point is, do we allow it to control our lives? Or do we turn to God for the strength and grace to do whatever we need to do, in spite of the fear?

As far as telling lies goes, there are some extreme occasions when Godly people do it. For example, Corrie ten Boom and her family told lies in order to hide Jews in their home and protect them from being murdered by the Nazis. However, they hated having to tell lies and they longed for the day when Hitler would be defeated by the Allies and such things would no longer be necessary.

According to the Bible, we don't fully know our own hearts. In order to have integrity, we need to keep repenting of known sins, and we also need to habitually invite God to search our hearts and show us if our actions or attitudes are sinful. David gave us a good example of this in the psalms:

> "Who can understand his errors? cleanse thou me from secret faults." (Psalm 19:12)

"Search me, O God, and know my heart: try me, and know my thoughts: And see if there be any wicked way in me, and lead me in the way everlasting." (Psalm 139:23-24)

May God give us the strength and wisdom and love to grow in integrity and in faithfulness to Him.

"Courage is fear that has said its prayers."

(Dorothy Bernard)

Chapter 21

Loving Difficult People

"If it be possible, as much as lieth in you, live peaceably with all men." (Romans 12:18)

Jesus said that the identifying mark of Christians should be their love. By "love" I mean Biblical love, as opposed to what the world calls love. Biblical love involves the entire person, and it doesn't come and go with the ebb and flow of emotions. It involves discipline and commitment, as opposed to being mushy. Jesus said:

> "By this shall all men know that ye are my disciples, if ye have love one to another." (John 13:35)

> "But I say unto you, Love your enemies, bless them that curse you, do good to them that hate you, and pray for them which despitefully use you, and persecute you; That ye may be the children of your Father which is in heaven: for he maketh his sun to rise on the evil and on the good, and sendeth rain on the just and on the unjust." (Matthew 5:44-45)

> "But I say unto you which hear, Love your enemies, do good to them which hate you, Bless them that curse you, and pray for them which despitefully use you." (Luke 6:27-28)

> "But love ye your enemies, and do good, and lend, hoping for nothing again; and your reward shall be great, and ye shall be the children of the Highest: for he is kind unto the

unthankful and to the evil. Be ye therefore merciful, as your Father also is merciful." (Luke 6:35-36)

Love tells the truth, even when it is unpleasant. An example is when Nathaniel confronted King David with his sin. Of course, we can tell the truth gently rather than roughly. But even then, some things are difficult to hear. And they are often precisely what we most need to hear:

"Faithful are the wounds of a friend; but the kisses of an enemy are deceitful." (Proverbs 27:6)

"But **speaking the truth in love**, may grow up into him in all things, which is the head, even Christ" (Ephesians 4:15, emphasis added)

Jesus loved us when we were rebellious sinners who deserved to go to hell. He was willing to die for us precisely when we least deserved it:

"For when we were yet without strength, in due time Christ died for the ungodly. For scarcely for a righteous man will one die: yet peradventure for a good man some would even dare to die. But God commendeth his love toward us, in that, while we were yet sinners, Christ died for us." (Romans 5:6-8)

Why should we love difficult people? Because God told us to, and if He is truly our Lord, then we need to obey Him. But also, because Jesus loves them. We do it for His sake. Not because they deserve it, but because Jesus deserves it.

Some people are so nasty that the only way that I can show them love is to pray for their salvation. But I can at least do that much, and it might make a difference. It's amazing what God can do.

For example, Chuck Colson was a ruthless politician who was known as Nixon's "hatchet man" and he became a Christian. The reason why he went to prison is because once he was a Christian, then he was no longer willing to tell lies in order to avoid going to prison. After he served his time, he started a ministry that helps prisoners come to know the Lord. They also help them after they are released. The convicts they work with have a very low rate of returning to prison.

God can reach some people who look like hopeless cases. For example, one of my Christian friends used to be a drug dealer and a satanist, and another used to be a member of Hells Angels. Both men have some problems, because sin leaves scars. But they love the Lord, and they are trying to live Biblically.

I heard the testimony of a man who had been a member of the Black Panthers before he became a Christian. He later became friends with a man who used to be a member of the KKK, until God opened his eyes and changed his heart. A former Black Panther and a former KKK member are now brothers in Christ. We serve an awesome God!

We are limited in our ability to judge people. Sometimes we think that they are good, when deep down inside they aren't. And sometimes we think that they are hopelessly lost, but deep down inside they are hungry for truth and looking for God. The Bible says:

> "...for the Lord seeth not as man seeth; for man looketh on the outward appearance, but the Lord looketh on the heart." (1 Samuel 16:7)

I often think of Betsy ten Boom, praying for the Nazi guards in Ravensbruck (the concentration camp where she and her sister Corrie were prisoners). We know that one of those guards became a Christian after the war. I wonder how many others did, but we never heard about it.

Remember the parable of the sower. (Matthew 13:3-23) The seed was good, so the results of the sowing depended on the quality of the soil. Some soil looked good, but there were rocks underneath it, and the plants died as soon as there was hardship. Some soil looked good, but there were weed seeds in it, and the weeds overcame the plants. Some soil looked good, and it was, and the plants thrived and bore fruit.

Similarly, some people look good, but there is hardness under the surface, and the Word of God cannot bear fruit in their lives. Conversely, some people look hopelessly bad, but there is something in them that responds to the Word of God. Like my friends the former satanist and the former Hells Angel, and the Nazi prison guard who became a Christian.

Like the sower in the parable, we should just sow love, and leave the results to God. No matter how bad people are, we can at least pray for their salvation. And we can have mercy on them. God has been merciful to us, and He told us to be merciful to others:

"Blessed are the merciful: for they shall obtain mercy." (Matthew 5:7)

"Be ye therefore merciful, as your Father also is merciful." (Luke 6:36)

If those people sin against us, then we can do what Stephen did while he was being stoned, and ask God not to hold that sin against them. God told us to forgive:

"And they stoned Stephen, calling upon God, and saying, Lord Jesus, receive my spirit. And he kneeled down, and cried with a loud voice, Lord, lay not this sin to their charge. And when he had said this, he fell asleep." (Acts 7:59-60)

The bottom line is love. And we can keep asking God to change our hearts and make us more loving:

> "Beloved, let us love one another: for love is of God; and every one that loveth is born of God, and knoweth God. He that loveth not knoweth not God; for God is love." (1 John 4:7-8)

> "As the Father hath loved me, so have I loved you: continue ye in my love." (John 15:9)

Oh the Deep Deep Love of Jesus
(by Samuel Frances, 1834-1925, public domain)

O the deep, deep love of Jesus,
Vast, unmeasured, boundless, free!
Rolling as a mighty ocean
In its fullness over me!
Underneath me, all around me,
Is the current of Thy love
Leading onward, leading homeward
To Thy glorious rest above!

O the deep, deep love of Jesus,
Spread His praise from shore to shore!
How He loveth, ever loveth,
Changeth never, nevermore!
How He watches o'er His loved ones,
Died to call them all His own;
How for them He intercedeth,
Watcheth o'er them from the throne!

O the deep, deep love of Jesus,
Love of every love the best!
'Tis an ocean vast of blessing,
'Tis a haven sweet of rest!
O the deep, deep love of Jesus,
'Tis a heaven of heavens to me;
And it lifts me up to glory,
For it lifts me up to Thee!

Chapter 22

The Antidote To Humanism

"For the time will come when they will not endure sound doctrine; but after their own lusts shall they heap to themselves teachers, having itching ears; And they shall turn away their ears from the truth, and shall be turned unto fables." (2 Timothy 4:3-4)

In Chapter 1, we saw how humanists oppose God so much that they are determined to change our culture and our moral values. One way that they have succeeded in doing this is by means of "fables." For modern Western society, this takes the form of fraudulent science. There are some scientists, anthropologists, and psychologists who claim to do research, but in reality they are attempting to do social engineering by means of lies that are dressed up in scientific vocabulary.

One example is Dr. Alfred Kinsey, the so-called "expert" whose "research" revolutionized people's thinking about sex. It encouraged the sexual revolution of the 1960s, and it led to sex education in public schools. It has also been used to justify the agenda of the radical homosexual activists.

Kinsey's "research" was fraudulent. Many of the adults that he interviewed and used for research were prisoners or prostitutes. That does **not** show the nature of the sexuality of most American adults.

In addition, his research included adults having sex with children, including infants. No matter how the children responded, Kinsey called it an orgasm. If they screamed, or sobbed, or went into spasms, or became unconscious, then Kinsey wrote it down as being an orgasm.

Where were the police when this was going on? Where was the public outcry about this sexual abuse of children? Why hasn't Dr. Kinsey been put in prison because it?

Dr. Judith Reisman has devoted years to exposing Kinsey and his fraudulent research. She wrote *Sexual Sabotage: How One Mad Scientist Unleashed a Plague of Corruption and Contagion on America*. She also wrote *Kinsey: Crimes and Consequences*, and she is a coauthor of *Kinsey, Sex and Fraud: The Indoctrination of a People*.

Margaret Mead's book *Coming of Age in Samoa* was also a fraud. It promoted the idea of cultural relativism and strongly encouraged the sexual revolution of the 1960s.[1]

For an excellent study of the many ways that humanist "experts" have deceived us in order to transform our culture and moral values, I recommend reading Ian T. Taylor's book *In the Minds of Men*. Taylor studied history, geology, medicine, and physics. His book deals with creation versus evolution, and other controversies.

Dr. Henry Morris' book *The Long War Against God* shows that evolution did not originate with Charles Darwin. He traces it back to the Greeks, Babylonians, and other ancient philosophers. He also shows how real science does not support evolution.

Henry Morris is the founder of the Institute for Creation Research (ICR). You can find a wealth of information at their website:

www.icr.org

The theory of evolution has had devastating practical consequences. For example, thousands of Australian Aborigines were murdered and their bodies were sent to museums because they were said to be a "missing link."[2] Hitler was inspired by Darwin. The Holocaust was Hitler's attempt to get rid of "inferior" races.[3] (See Appendix B, "Darwin's Deadly Legacy.")

From Genesis to the Book of Revelation, the Bible makes it absolutely clear that God is our Creator. Here are three of the numerous Scripture passages about this:

"All things were made by him; and without him was not any thing made that was made." (John 1:3)

"God, who at sundry times and in divers manners spake in time past unto the fathers by the prophets, Hath in these last days spoken unto us by his Son, whom he hath appointed heir of all things, **by whom also he made the worlds**; Who being the brightness of his glory, and the express image of his person, and **upholding all things by the word of his power**, when he had by himself purged our sins, sat down on the right hand of the Majesty on high" (Hebrews 1:1-3, emphasis added)

"Thou art worthy, O Lord, to receive glory and honour and power: for thou hast created all things, and for thy pleasure they are and were created." (Revelation 4:11)

Taking Responsibility for Our Lives

I know a psychologist who really helps people, but the reason is that he believes the Bible, he loves the people, and he has good common sense. In other words, for him, Biblical truth and morality trump what he was taught in his psychology classes.

Unfortunately, that is quite rare. As a result, psychologists can wind up doing more harm than good. Hitler and Stalin used psychology to undermine Christian morality and manipulate people. In addition, the techniques of mind control and "social engineering" are based on psychology.

Freud and Jung are the founders of modern psychology. Sigmund Freud was an atheist. He hated religion, especially Christianity and Judaism. Freud was obsessed with sex, and he tried to justify gross immorality.[4] Carl Jung was an occultist who was led by "spirit guides" (i.e., demons).[5] Therefore, it should not be surprising that psychology has some foundational problems.

Psychology basically denies that people are responsible for their own behavior. It often attributes bad behavior to things that happened to people in the past. It also blames present pressures, or things that people lack, such as finances, education, or self esteem.

That foundational assumption is not true. There are some good, Godly people who came out of horrible backgrounds. Instead of following in the footsteps of the people who did bad things to them, they were determined to do just the opposite. And they succeeded.

People are not like driftwood, which gets pulled along by every current that influences it. On the contrary, people are like swimmers. They can decide to go in a particular direction in spite of the pull of the current.

There is an old comedian whose name I can't recall. He said that the neighborhood that he grew up in was so bad that everybody who came out of there became a gangster, a policeman, or a priest. That is a good illustration of the point. People who have been through terrible things can love and forgive. Instead of becoming bitter, they can become compassionate and try to help others.

The best book for helping us psychologically is the Bible. It tells us to forgive those who hurt us, to repent for our sins, and to love one another. If we want to know how to love in practical terms, the Gospels and Epistles give good, solid, practical examples to emulate and instructions to follow. Here is one of them:

> "Charity [love] suffereth long, and is kind; charity envieth not; charity vaunteth not itself, is not puffed up, Doth not behave itself unseemly, seeketh not her own, is not easily

provoked, thinketh no evil; Rejoiceth not in iniquity, but rejoiceth in the truth" (1 Corinthians 13:4-6)

If we live Biblically, we may still have some emotional issues. However, there will be a huge difference in degree. For example, it can make the difference between normal discouragement and suicidal despair. Or we might find ourselves thinking something nasty about somebody, and then repent of those thoughts, instead of doing bad things to that person.

No matter what our circumstances, God's grace will be sufficient for us. (2 Corinthians 12:9) He will enable us to endure, persevere, and live more Biblically. And He will make everything work out for our long-term, eternal good, because we love Him. (Romans 8:28)

We will never be fully right in our thinking and emotions until we see Jesus Christ face to face. And what a wonderful day that will be!

"Beloved, now are we the sons of God, and it doth not yet appear what we shall be: but we know that, when he shall appear, we shall be like him; for we shall see him as he is." (1 John 3:2)

*"That at the name of Jesus
every knee should bow,
of things in heaven, and things in earth,
and things under the earth;
And that every tongue should confess that
Jesus Christ is Lord,
to the glory of God the Father."*
(Philippians 2:10-11)

Chapter 23

A Biblical Approach to Pain

"And we know that all things work together for good to them that love God, to them who are the called according to his purpose." (Romans 8:28)

How should we deal with pain and hardship? There are no easy answers, no formulas. Everyone has to work it out for themselves. Dealing with suffering can be extremely difficult, but with God's help, it is possible.

We need to be wary of the pat answers that are sometimes given. They usually do not work. Job's "comforters" gave him pat answers, and God said of them, "You have not spoken of me the thing which is right." (Job 42:8)

One pat answer is that suffering is always the result of sin, so the way to deal with it is to discover and get rid of the sin. It is well to examine ourselves and see if there is sin that needs to be dealt with. But suffering is not always caused by sin.

Jesus was sinless; yet he suffered terribly. Paul suffered much. Can we say that this was because of sin he had not dealt with?

Christians have been persecuted and martyred from the First Century until today. Would anyone suggest that this is because of sin?

Another pat answer is that, if our prayer to be relieved of suffering is not answered, it must be because of lack of faith. We do need to pray, believing. (James 1:6) There have been times when I was going through difficulties and realized that I lacked faith, and was able to do something about it. But lack of faith is not the only reason why men endure suffering.

A Biblical Approach to Pain

The prophets who suffered in terrible ways were commended for their faith. (Hebrews 11:32-40) When God refused to heal Paul's "thorn in the flesh," He said nothing about a lack of faith. Rather, He said,

> "My grace is sufficient for thee: for my strength is made perfect in weakness." (2 Corinthians 12:9)

God did not answer Jesus' prayer that He not have to endure the Crucifixion. (Matthew 26:36-42) Would anyone suggest that it was because of a lack of faith?

Many American Christians are so used to comfort and safety and security that they fail to realize what life is like for Christians in third world countries, and in countries with serious persecution. In contrast, the Bible tells us that it is normal to have to face serious difficulties. That we should be prepared to face at least one "evil day," which implies that some people will face many of them.

> "Beloved, think it not strange concerning the fiery trial which is to try you, as though some strange thing happened unto you: But rejoice, inasmuch as ye are partakers of Christ's sufferings; that, when his glory shall be revealed, ye may be glad also with exceeding joy." (1 Peter 4:12-13)

> "Yea, and all that will live godly in Christ Jesus shall suffer persecution." (2 Timothy 3:12)

> "Put on the whole armour of God, that ye may be able to stand against the wiles of the devil. For we wrestle not against flesh and blood, but against principalities, against powers, against the rulers of the darkness of this world, against spiritual wickedness in high places. Wherefore take unto you the whole armour of God, that ye may be

able to withstand **in the evil day**, and having done all, to stand." (Ephesians 6:11-13, emphasis added)

Here are some Biblical principles that are helpful when facing such things.

Have the Right Attitude

Underlying everything else is the attitude with which we deal with pain, suffering and difficulties when they come, as they will to most of us. I can identify three general kinds of attitudes.

First, when suffering, difficulties, or hardships come, we say, "Why me?" We dwell on the seeming injustice and unfairness of it. This easily leads to self-pity, to feeling sorry for ourselves, which is one of the devil's most effective schemes for making a Christian ineffective. From there it can go on to blaming God for allowing the suffering, and to anger and bitterness at God. Ultimately, this can, in some cases, lead to a total turning away from God, a total rejection of God.

This approach can be very damaging, very destructive. It does nothing to relieve the suffering or make it easier to bear.

Many of us go through the early stages of this approach for a while when suffering or difficulties come. But if we stay there, and do not move on, the result can be very destructive to us.

Second, we can decide to take a constructive attitude. We can say, "God, this suffering, this difficulty, is here. I don't like it, but I need to accept it. What are you trying to teach me by it? How can I use it to grow? How can I bring good out of it?"

With this approach, we can turn the suffering, the difficulty, to our good. We can use it to increase in maturity and strength. We get our mind off our suffering and onto God and what he is doing in our lives. If we can see some good purpose in the suffering, it becomes easier to handle.

There is a third approach which builds on the second and is even better. Paul asked that he might "know him [Jesus], and the power of his resurrection, and the fellowship of his sufferings." (Philippians 3:10)

What does this mean? I am not sure. I am not there and have not experienced what Paul is talking about. But I suggest that Paul is saying that, when suffering comes, we can see it as a means of drawing closer to Jesus.

As we suffer, we can begin to understand better what Jesus voluntarily suffered for us, and appreciate more fully what he did for us. As we are unjustly treated, we can begin to understand more fully the rejection, injustice and false accusations that Jesus continually suffered. We can become more like Jesus, which is the goal of our transformation.

A related concept is found in 2 Corinthians 1:4-5, where Paul says that God "comforteth us in all our tribulation, that we may be able to comfort them which are in any trouble, by the comfort wherewith we ourselves are comforted of God. For as the sufferings of Christ abound in us, so our consolation also aboundeth by Christ."

Those who have lost a spouse can understand what others are going through who have lost a spouse; they can speak to them in a way that others cannot. Those who have been physically or sexually abused can understand what others are going through who have suffered abuse. Those who have endured physical pain can understand what others are going through who have to deal with physical pain. And so on.

Our own suffering enables us to minister more effectively to others who are suffering. Thus our suffering helps to bring us together more closely as the body of Christ. It helps us comfort and encourage our brothers and sisters in Christ, and to "edify one another" (build each other up). (1 Thessalonians 5:11)

Once we have taken care of our attitude, there are some other specific things we can do.

Accept Hardship

Pain and hardship occur. They are part of this world. No one is immune or exempt from them. There is no guarantee that they will not occur. When they come in our life, we need to be able to accept them. As Peter wrote,

> "Beloved, think it not strange concerning the fiery trial which is to try you, as though some strange thing happened unto you" (1 Peter 4:12)

This is not easy, but it is essential.

The Bible tells us to go further, and to "count it all joy" when trials come. (James 1:2) I confess that I am not yet at this point! But if we can see pain and suffering as experiences from which we can learn and grow, then perhaps we can begin to see them as things that God is using for our good, and be able to rejoice in them.

Decide to Overcome

The Bible says that, in God's power, we can be overcomers. We need to come to a decision to believe those Scripture passages. We need to make a conscious decision that, with God's help, we can and will overcome the pain and suffering. We need to decide that we will not allow it to undermine our faith in God, our joy, our peace, or our ability to function.

Do What You Can

Paul said,

> "Wherefore take unto you the whole armour of God, that ye may be able to withstand in the evil day, and **having done all**, to stand" (Ephesians 6:13, emphasis added)

He was talking about facing the devil, but I think the principle applies to every kind of adversity. God wants us to do everything we can.

In the case of pain and suffering, this means to get all the help you can. Medical science knows quite a lot about pain management. What they have to offer does not always work, does not always work fully, and sometimes has side effects we prefer to avoid, but we might as well use it when we can.

Having a prayer partner, or a close friend in whom you can confide, can be very helpful. Prayer is always helpful. So is reading, studying, and reflecting on the Bible.

My point is, avail yourself of anything that will be genuinely helpful in relieving your pain. There is no virtue in unnecessary suffering.

There are, however, some techniques of pain relief that Christians should avoid. Two examples are hypnosis (which involves allowing someone else to manipulate your mind while you are not aware of what he is doing) and New Age forms of meditation (which originate in pagan religions). Anything that derives from, or involves, a pagan religion should be avoided by Christians. There is little sense in relieving physical pain at the cost of spiritual harm to yourself!

Pray

One of the things we can always do, and one of the first things we should do, is to pray.

"Is any among you afflicted? Let him pray." (James 5:13)

Prayer brings us in touch with the almighty power of God. God does not always take us out of difficult circumstances. But he is with us in them. He is "a very present help **in** trouble." (Psalm 46:1, emphasis added)

"Yea, though I walk through the valley of the shadow of death, I will fear no evil: for thou art with me; thy rod and thy staff they comfort me." (Psalm 23:4)

Prayer also takes our mind off of our circumstances and puts it on God.

Focus on God and Not Our Circumstances

Paul, who went through a remarkable amount of suffering, wrote that in all circumstances we should give thanks. (1 Thessalonians 5:18) Our thanks do not depend on the circumstances. Our thanks depend on who God is, on the salvation he has so freely given us, and on the relationship we have with Him. As Paul wrote,

> "For our light affliction, which is but for a moment, worketh for us a far more exceeding and eternal weight of glory; While we look not at the things which are seen, but at the things which are not seen: for the things which are seen are temporal; but the things which are not seen are eternal." (2 Corinthians 4:17-18)

To Paul, five whippings, three beatings with rods, stoning, and many other hardships were a "light affliction," which was just for a moment! This seems amazing. But when we compare all that Paul suffered during some 60 years on earth to the joy of spending eternity in Heaven with God, it becomes quite minor.

Because our thanksgiving does not depend on the circumstances, we are not at the mercy of the circumstances. I think this is what Paul was talking about when he said that he had learned how to be content in every situation. (Philippians 4:12) We shouldn't focus too much on the situation. We need to look at God. It is by this, also, that we can achieve "the peace of God, which passeth all understanding." (Philippians 4:7)

Our faith and hope also need to rise above our circumstances. Abraham "believed in hope." (Romans 4:18) All the circumstances gave Abraham reason to believe that he and Sarah could not have a child. But against that expectation based on his situation, Abraham set his hope, his confident expectation, based on God's promise to him. He went past all the natural circumstances to believe God's promise.

Whatever our situation, we need to believe that God is bigger than anything that we face, that he will enable us to bear it, and that he will bring us through it. Whatever our circumstances, we need to believe that God will strengthen us with all power according to His glorious might, so that we may have great endurance and patience. (Colossians 1:11)

In painful situations, many have found that it helps to focus on God. Jesus endured the Cross "for the joy that was set before him." (Hebrews 12:2) He looked at God's power and His promise rather than looking at his own physical agony.

Stephen, while being stoned, had a vision of heaven with Jesus standing at the right hand of God. (Acts 7:55-56) After Paul and Silas were beaten with rods and put in stocks in the inner prison, they prayed and sang hymns to God, and God moved mightily on their behalf. (Acts 16:25)

The Christian martyrs in the Roman arena sang hymns as they faced the wild beasts who were about to eat them. Many other martyrs have faced their martyrdom with praise to God.

Let God Bring Good out of Our Situation

There is a further reason to focus on God rather than the circumstances. God works for good in all things, even in the most unlikely situations. (Romans 8:28) We can praise God, pray, read our Bible, reflect on Scripture passages. Whatever works for us. Whatever helps us draw closer to God and see things more from His perspective. Turn our situation over to Him in prayer. Ask

Him to deal with us and to show us anything He wants to show us about it.

> "Draw nigh to God and he will draw nigh to you." (James 4:8)

We should be honest with God. He can handle anger, frustration, and even discouragement and despair. Job complained and got angry at God. And God spoke to him at length, revealed Himself to him, and said that Job had "spoken of me [God] the thing which is right." (Job 42:8)

David often complained and poured out his heart to God. And God called him "a man after mine own heart." (Acts 13:22) God does not mind hearing the distress and even anger of one who is genuinely seeking after Him.

Remain Faithful to God

Job asked the question that many of us ask when suffering comes. He said,

> "...shall we receive good at the hand of God, and shall we not receive evil?" (Job 2:10)

Do we love God for what he gives us, or for who he is? Can we love Him and serve Him even in suffering? Even if he seems to have deserted us? Even if he seems not to answer our prayers?

In His great end-time prophecy, Jesus told the disciples that they would be persecuted and put to death. He said that many people would turn away from the faith, and the love of many would grow cold. (See Matthew 24:3-14.) Jesus ended by saying,

> "But he that shall endure unto the end, the same shall be saved." (Matthew 24:13)

In each of the letters to the churches in the Book of Revelation, there is a promise of blessings to the one who overcomes. God has promised that we can be more than conquerors. (Romans 8:37) "For whatsoever is born of God overcometh the world." (1 John 5:4)

God has made it possible to overcome pain and suffering, no matter how severe and prolonged.

May God bless us all as we seek to live according to His Word!

> For which cause we faint not;
> but though our outward man perish,
> yet the inward man is renewed day by day.
> For our light affliction, which is but for a moment,
> worketh for us a far more exceeding and
> eternal weight of glory;
> While we look not at the things which are seen,
> but at the things which are not seen;
> for the things which are seen are temporal,
> but the things which are not seen are eternal.
> (2 Corinthians 4:16-18)

Faithful Friend
(By Maria Kneas)

Jesus, You're the friend who'll never leave me.
You're the friend who'll always understand.
You will not forsake me or deceive me.
You'll stay by my side until the end.

When I'm afraid, You'll put Your arm around me.
You're the faithful friend who's tried and true.
No matter what the troubles that surround me
You will find a way to get me through.

Your love is strong, it's deeper than the ocean.
It's higher than the moon and stars above.
When earth and stars are gone and time has ended,
I'll still live, rejoicing in Your love.

Light After Darkness
(By Francis Ridley Havergal)

Light after darkness, gain after loss,
Strength after suffering, crown after cross.
Sweet after bitter, song after sigh,
Home after wandering, praise after cry.

Sheaves after sowing, sun after rain,
Sight after mystery, peace after pain.
Joy after sorrow, calm after blast,
Rest after weariness, sweet rest at last.

Near after distant, gleam after gloom,
Love after loneliness, life after tomb.
After long agony, rapture of bliss!
Right was the pathway leading to this!

(Public domain)

Chapter 24

The Big Picture — Eternity

*"**Looking unto Jesus** the author and finisher of our faith; who **for the joy that was set before him** endured the cross, despising the shame, and is set down at the right hand of the throne of God." (Hebrews 12:2, emphasis added)*

The Apostle Paul endured great hardship and suffering. He went through many traumatic experiences but he called them a "light affliction" that was only "for a moment." (2 Corinthians 4:17)

How was he able to do that? He was looking at the greatness of God and the glory of Eternity. He had some understanding of Heaven. He had been "caught up to the third heaven," into "paradise," where he heard amazing things that he was not allowed to tell us about. (2 Corinthians 12:2-4)

We need to focus on the really big picture—on Almighty God, and His amazing love for us, and on spending Eternity with Him in Heaven. If we do that, then we will be able to endure traumatic things, but still have peace and joy in spite of them:

"And the peace of God, which passeth all understanding, shall keep your hearts and minds through Christ Jesus." (Philippians 4:7)

"...the joy of the Lord is your strength." (Nehemiah 8:10)

We are not capable of comprehending how much God loves us, and the wonderful things that He has prepared for us. The Book of Revelation gives us a few brief glimpses of the joy in Heaven, but we won't really understand it until we get there:

"But as it is written, Eye hath not seen, nor ear heard, neither have entered into the heart of man, the things which God hath prepared for them that love him." (1 Corinthians 2:9)

God calls us children. Because they are young and lack experience, children don't understand the real value of things. They can shred paper money to use as nesting material for their pet gerbil, or draw pictures on the walls, or play catch with priceless china. Last year, a Ming Dynasty vase sold for over a million dollars, but a child wouldn't understand something like that. To him, it would just be another object to play with. It's similar to a puppy using your best shoes as a chew toy.

What God has waiting for us is far greater than we can possibly understand now. However, God has been revealing things about it throughout history, beginning with Job, which is one of the oldest books in the Bible. He also told the Prophet Daniel about the Resurrection of the dead:

"For I know that my redeemer liveth, and that he shall stand at the latter day upon the earth: And though after my skin worms destroy this body, yet in my flesh shall I see God: Whom I shall see for myself, and mine eyes shall behold, and not another; though my reins be consumed within me." (Job 19:25-27)

"And many of them that sleep in the dust of the earth shall awake, some to everlasting life, and some to shame and everlasting contempt. And they that be wise shall shine as the brightness of the firmament; and they that turn many to righteousness as the stars for ever and ever." (Daniel 12:2-3)

We are going to be wonderfully changed. When we see the Lord Jesus Christ face to face, then we will become like He is. Finally our minds and our emotions will work right, and we will see things from God's perspective. Finally we will be totally free from all sin and sefishness. We will be pure and holy and overflowing with love, like Jesus. This transformation will be so radical that we cannot comprehend it now:

> "Beloved, now are we the sons of God, and it doth not yet appear what we shall be: but we know that, when he shall appear, we shall be like him; for we shall see him as he is." (1 John 3:2)

We are not the only ones who will be changed. The entire world will be transformed. And not just our world, but the entire universe:

> "Nevertheless we, according to his promise, look for new heavens and a new earth, wherein dwelleth righteousness." (2 Peter 3:13)

We were horrified by seeing 45 Christians in the Middle East paraded in cages before being burned alive. They were mocked and scorned. They were probably hungry, thirsty, and very frightened while they were in those cages, knowing that the overwhelming heat and pain of fire would soon be upon them. But look where those martyrs are now, as they rejoice in Heaven, and look at how tender and loving God is with them:

> "They shall hunger no more, neither thirst any more; neither shall the sun light on them, nor any heat. For the Lamb which is in the midst of the throne shall feed them, and shall lead them unto living fountains of waters: and God shall wipe away all tears from their eyes." (Revelation 7:16-17)

"And they sing the song of Moses the servant of God, and the song of the Lamb, saying, Great and marvellous are thy works, Lord God Almighty; just and true are thy ways, thou King of saints. Who shall not fear thee, O Lord, and glorify thy name? for thou only art holy: for all nations shall come and worship before thee; for thy judgments are made manifest." (Revelation 15:3-4)

Even Christians who do not have to endure martyrdom suffer many things. Some have illnesses that cause tremendous physical pain. Others have lives filled with overwhelming heartaches. All of us have to endure fear and heartbreak and pain and grief. But that is not the end of the story. Look at what is waiting for us in Heaven:

"And God shall wipe away all tears from their eyes; and there shall be no more death, neither sorrow, nor crying, neither shall there be any more pain: for the former things are passed away. And he that sat upon the throne said, Behold, I make all things new." (Revelation 21:4-5)

I SAW YOU SEATED
(by Frances Morrisson) (My Mom)

Through the prophet's eye
I saw You seated
focus to explosions of jewelled light
and thundering flashings
coupled with the rushing sounds of waters
causing prophet's tongue to stumble,
causing trembling knees to seek in weakness
the humbling fact of earth.

O holy, holy, holi-ness,
crowns of gold, tossing, tossing;
clouds of saints adoring.

Holy, holy, holi-ness;
flashes of Ox, of Eagle;
flashes of Man and Lion.

Holy, holy, holi-ness;
the flow of gold-transparent
flowing from the throne.

O holy, holy, holi-ness,
    angels hovering, angels singing,
    prayers as incense rising, rising.
Holy, holy, holiness.

And we, O Lord, not prophets of old but saints of now
straddling earth and heaven,
embrace Your Cross, exultantly;
trust in You,
obedient,
and give assent for all that is to be.

Chapter 25

The Challenge

The first part of *Prepare for Persecution* ("We Are Living in Perilous Times") gives valuable information. It's an overview from a variety of perspectives—historical, political, social engineering (i.e., brainwashing), and spiritual.

However, the second part of the book ("Biblical Encouragement and Guidance") is very different. It gives Biblical principles for living that will strengthen and encourage Christians. This will help equip them to stand firm in their faith and be faithful to God no matter what happens.

It would be wise to read that second part of the book slowly and carefully and prayerfully. As you read, take time to think about it, and find ways to put it into practice in your daily life.

You might want to read that part of the book several times, in order to get the full impact of the Scriptures and the Bibical principles. Sometimes when I'm facing challenges, I reread it myself. (There are times when we need to be reminded about things that we already learned.)

Look at what Jesus said in Matthew chapter 7. This applies to **His** words, not mine. If you ignore what I said and just study the Scripture passages that I quoted, then this applies to them:

> "Therefore whosoever heareth these sayings of mine, and doeth them, I will liken him unto a wise man, which built his house upon a rock: And the rain descended, and the floods came, and the winds blew, and beat upon that house; and it fell not: for it was founded upon a rock. And every one that heareth these sayings of mine, and doeth them not, shall be likened unto a foolish man, which built his house upon the sand: And the rain descended, and the

floods came, and the winds blew, and beat upon that house; and it fell: and great was the fall of it." (Matthew 7:24-27)

Persecution is discouraging. So are health problems, difficult relationships, and financial problems. That's why I wrote the book *How to Fight Discouragement*. It gives practical ways to apply Biblical principles to our lives so that we can trust God at a deeper level and live more Biblically in all areas of our life. Then we will find God's peace, strength, comfort, and encouragement in spite of the storms.

I've been going through some difficult situations lately, and I've been helped by the book. Even when we know things, when the pressure is on, we need to be reminded about them.

If you get *How to Fight Discouragement* and work with the Biblical principles in that book, then you will be better prepared to stand firm in your faith in spite of persecution. You will also be better equipped to help others get to know God better and trust Him more. For nonbelievers, that could lead to their salvation. For Christians, that will enable them to become stronger, more faithful Christians in spite of the increasingly perilous times in which we are living.

Jesus wants us to be "the light of the world." (Matthew 5:14) Therefore, as the world grows darker, we need to shine more brightly.

Chapter 26

Helping Others Stand Firm

Please consider giving *Prepare for Persecution* to your pastor. Christians need to get spiritually and emotionally prepared **now**, while we are still in the early stages of persecution. And their pastors should help them do it.

Unfortunately, many pastors don't understand the degree of persecution that is already happening. They need to know now, so that they can help their people strengthen their faith and their level of commitment to God.

In the face of persecution, all Christians need to be equipped to respond Biblically instead of reacting carnally. Pastors should help their people become prepared for those challenges. They need to do it **now**, because we are already in the early stages of persecution, and it is ramping up.

We Christians need to get spiritually and emotionally prepared for the storm **before** it hits. We need to develop enough spiritual backbone to be able to stand firm in our faith and "endure to the end."

Please consider giving *Prepare for Persecution* to friends and family members in order to help them get prepared. If you think that the idea of persecution would be overwhelming for them, then you could give them *How to Fight Discouragement* instead.

Once they read *How to Fight Discouragement*, and work with the Biblical principles that it discusses, then they should become stronger, more mature Christians. That would enable them to be able to think about persecution, and want to prepare for it both spiritually and emotionally.

Both books discuss practical ways of applying various Biblical principles to our lives, and they both quote a lot of Scripture. In addition, *Prepare for Persecution* also talks about some of the problems that we are facing. Because that information is thoroughly documented, your friends and family members should be willing to take it seriously.

The people you are close to need to get prepared **NOW**. **Before** the storm hits. They cannot afford to be blindsided.

It takes time to get Scripture into us to the point that it influences our thoughts and actions on a moment-to-moment basis. It takes time to develop our "trust muscles" and our "forgiveness muscles." It takes time to become mature Christians who have enough depth of commitment and strength of conviction to be able to live the way that Jesus wants us to live.

The first part of *Prepare for Persecution* shows that our Constitutional freedoms are under attack, occultism is becoming more and more mainstream, and Christians are being subjected to lawsuits and threatened with prison for living according to their moral beliefs. Life is becoming more difficult for committed Christians, and unless God intervenes, this will probably increase.

Therefore, we need to get spiritually and emotionally prepared **NOW**, before more serious challenges come. And so do those we love.

It is my hope and prayer that *How to Fight Discouragement* and the second part of *Prepare for Persecution* will help you do that. When I get to Heaven, I want to meet people who tell me that I helped them get there.

I know of one for sure, and that's my husband Ray. God used many things to bring Ray to salvation, and I was privileged to be one of them.

May God use all of us to help others make it to Heaven.

Appendix A

Goddess Worship In America

> *"'Has a nation ever changed its gods? (Yet they are not gods at all.) But my people have exchanged their Glory for worthless idols. Be appalled at this, O heavens, and shudder with great horror,' declares the LORD. 'My people have committed two sins: They have forsaken me, the spring of living water, and have dug their own cisterns, broken cisterns that cannot hold water.'"*
> *(Jeremiah 2:11-13)*

The worship of pagan goddesses is most obvious with Wiccans. However, it is also common in universities and nursing schools. It is promoted by the media and is a component of New Age feminism. It has infiltrated mainline denominational churches and its influence can be felt throughout our society.

This movement is impacting our culture, and especially the younger generation. One troubling aspect of it is that, according to some of its proponents, facts and logic are "patriarchal" and therefore they are irrelevant. As you will see, some so-called scholars openly say that it is alright to make things up and present them as if they were historical facts.

Philip G. Davis is a professor of religious studies at the University of Prince Edward Island in Canada. He wrote the book *Goddess Unmasked* because he saw that goddess worship was being taken seriously in religious institutions, and that myths about the goddess were being taught as factual history on campus. Most of the information in this appendix comes from his book.

Creating a Goddess-Friendly Culture

The "Age of Enlightenment" gave birth to rationalist materialism. In reaction against this denial of the importance of emotions, a generation of Romantic poets, novelists, artists, musicians and philosophers developed. Many of them were involved with drugs, the occult, Rosicrucianism, or Freemasonry.

Following Darwin's theory of evolution, they speculated wildly about the evolution of society. Nationalism became a romantic search for pagan roots, as seen in Wagner's operas and the fairy tales researched by the Brothers Grimm. Womanhood was idealized. The myth of a past utopian matriarchy was developed. Psychologist Carl Jung idealized the concept of the "*anima*," the feminine side of man.[1]

Romanticism even invaded history and archaeology. Bachoven developed a theory of matriarchy which was openly based on imagination, and not on searching for hard facts. Feminist scholars followed Bachoven's lead. A historic myth was developed in which an ideal, matriarchal, goddess-worshipping society was destroyed by patriarchal invaders who brought with them all the ills of modern society.[2]

The scholarship involved in these studies of history and archaeology is so faulty that Philip Davis says:

> "An important lesson of this book is the ease with which patent falsehoods may clothe themselves in the garb of scholarship and masquerade as truth."[3]

Some feminist "scholars" and other academic radicals openly say that objective facts and historical accuracy are not even a valid goal:

> "A feminist scholar told her audience that it is indeed 'ethical' for an historian to ignore historical evidence in

order to construct a narrative... while still presenting it as history." [4]

In addition to "constructing narratives" (i.e., making up stories and presenting it as history), there are many academic radicals who "explicitly reject the quest for objective truth; they claim that objectivity is not only impossible to achieve in pure form, but actually illegitimate in the first place because it expresses a patriarchal, oppressive mentality." [5]

Before full-blown goddess worship developed in the 1950s, American art showed that popular imagination was being prepared for it. For example, the Statue of Liberty looks like a Greek goddess and is over three hundred feet high. The inscription presents the statue as speaking, and she calls herself "Mother of Exiles." [6]

A 1915 poster for the Red Cross shows an American nurse with a billowing, hooded cape that makes her look like a cross between a nurse and a Greek goddess. She carries a placard which says:

> "I am the Red Cross of Peace. I heal the wounds of war. I am a refuge from fire, flood and pestilence. The love of little children is mine." [7]

The National Academy of Sciences has a Great Hall done in Byzantine architecture that was designed to look like a "temple of science." The dome of that hall looks like it belongs in a cathedral, except that it has figures that look like Greek goddesses. Science is personified as a goddess, with an inscription that says:

> "To science, pilot of industry, conquerer of disease, multiplier of the harvest, explorer of the universe, revealer of nature's laws, eternal guide to truth." [8]

The Wiccan Goddess

Wicca was developed in England by Gerald B. Gardner, who was the first fully public witch of modern times. He was a spiritualist, a Freemason, and a Rosicrucian, with an extensive background in the occult.

Gardner was a member of the Golden Dawn. Aleister Crowley (a satanist) initiated Gardner into the fourth degree of the O.T.O. (Ordo Templi Orientis). Gardner was acquainted with a witch named "old Dorothy Fordham" and claimed to have been initiated into a coven. He used various occult texts in developing his rituals, including texts that were written by Aleister Crowley.[9]

Aiden Kelley, a Wiccan trained in biblical criticism, applied his critical skills to Gardner's archive. Based on Kelley's findings, Philip Davis concludes that:

> "First, [Kelly's] identification of Gardner's literary sources leaves little doubt that Gardner's own witchcraft texts were his personal creation and not something handed on to him from an ancient tradition" [10]

Therefore, it is difficult to know how much Gardner's Wicca resembles ancient witchcraft.

Doreen Valiente was Gardner's High Priestess. She was informed enough to spot the passages from Crowley in the rituals, and she rewrote them so that Crowley's name would not discourage potential inquirers.

Initially, the male, horned god and the High Priest were preeminent. By the mid-1960s, the goddess was the supreme deity in Wicca, and ritual authority was vested in the High Priestess.[11]

Through Wicca, goddess worship has now infiltrated our American culture:

"The appearance of the Goddess in other radical feminist circles, and then in churches and universities, did not occur until after the establishment of modern witchcraft as a viable new religion." [12]

"Goddess spirituality seems well on the way to becoming the most successful of all these neopagan manifestations in the English-speaking world." [13]

Wicca presents itself as a wholesome worship of a gentle, benevolent goddess. It's motto is, "An ye do none harm do what ye will." However, in real life the results of Wicca are not wholesome at all.

William Schnoebelen and his wife Sharon were High Priest and High Priestess of their coven, and they believed that they were doing a good thing. However, rivalry developed with another coven, and the witches put curses on one another. Several of their witches became drug addicts. Most of their witches had their marriages destroyed.[14]

The Goddess and Mainline Churches

In November 1993, a Re-imagining Conference was held in Minneapolis. Most of the 2,000 participants were women.

This was an ecumenical church conference attended by Presbyterians, Methodists, Lutherans, Roman Catholics, and members of almost a dozen other denominations. They invoked Sophia, the goddess of Wisdom, calling her their Creator. Prayers and liturgies were addressed to this goddess. Communion consisted of milk and honey instead of bread and wine.

They openly rejected the doctrines of the Incarnation and the Atonement. Christian lesbians were applauded for coming out of the closet. They encouraged "sex among friends" as a norm.

This conference was initiated by, sponsored by, and attended by representatives of the major American churches:[15]

"Re-imagining was an unprecedented event: an inter-denominational assembly of Christians openly bent on destroying the historic Christian religion root and branch, and steering the churches into wholesale neopaganism." [16]

Neopagan and Wiccan themes are amazingly prominent within older religious establishments. One reason for this is the quest for "inclusive" language and the attempt to apply more female imagery to God. Liturgy reform and revised hymnals have featured feminine imagery and metaphors for God the Mother.[17]

The Unitarian-Universalist church developed a ten-session workshop on feminism which encourages goddess worship and even endorses witchcraft. This workshop is called *Cakes for the Queen of Heaven*. It has been circulated through the major denominations and adopted for use in many mainstream churches.[18]

The following quotation from Jeremiah gives God's perspective about this:

"Do you not see what they are doing in the towns of Judah and in the streets of Jerusalem? The children gather wood, the fathers light the fire, and the women knead the dough and make **cakes of bread for the Queen of Heaven**. They pour out drink offerings to other gods to provoke me to anger." (Jeremiah 7:16-18, emphasis added)

A Canadian television station ran a five-part series titled *Return of the Goddess*, which introduced many people to goddess worship. The National Film Board of Canada produced *Goddess Remembered*, which became one of their most popular productions ever, being featured by public broadcasting TV stations in the United States as well as in Canada. *Cakes for the Queen of Heaven* and *Goddess Remembered* have both become staples for study groups in some major denominations.[19]

The Goddess and the University

The credibility of goddess worship has been increased by its acceptance by university professors and its incorporation into textbooks:[20]

> "[T]he doctrines of a new religion are being packaged and promoted as factual material for use in publicly funded and accredited institutions of higher education." [21]

The broader plans of gender feminism seem to have been most fully articulated, promoted and implemented among academics. Some feminists have even demanded that the goddess be given parity with the God of the Bible in university religion programs. This will impact our entire society because universities and colleges are training most of our future leaders, including government, health care, and the clergy:[22]

> "[R]adical professors are... using the classroom for recruitment, turning students into political activists. The campus, therefore, is a natural place to look for signs of the radical feminist New Age as it emerges." [23]

The Goddess and Health Care

Goddess worship has become strong in the field of health care, particularly nursing. Health care professionals are actively promoting New Age practices. For example, "therapeutic touch" (passing one's hands above a patient's body in order to manipulate auras and energy fields) has reportedly been taught to thousands of nurses in eighty North American nursing programs.[24]

Goddess worship has been overtly promoted, as can be seen from the following quotation from the National League for Nursing, which is an accrediting agency for nursing schools:

"Women's wisdom is ageless and timeless, and passes from generation to generation primarily by oral tradition.... These origins are grounded in women's experiences, female symbolism, and the spiritual roots of the Triple Goddess." [25]

Wiccan Indoctrination in Public Schools

Ron Campbell's ministry (The Jeremiah Project) deals with the occult. It discusses ways in which occultism has gained widespread acceptance in America. One of these ways is through the public school system. He says:

"*Impressions*, a curriculum used in many school districts, instructs teachers and students in how to cast spells.... Another curriculum called *Duso the Dolphin* employs relaxation techniques and sends hypnotized youngsters off on guided fantasies" [26]

The children are told to **chant** the spells. Their teachers require them to role play being magicians or sorcerers or witches, and chant spells. This is enforced training in practical witchcraft, paid for by U.S. tax dollars.

Duso the Dolphin and another popular curriculum called *Pumsey the Dragon* use relaxation techniques that are "identical to those used in hypnosis." In other words, they hypnotize the students.

What Can We Do?

We need to be informed so that we can help people we know who have become confused by these things. Also, we should take the following Scriptures seriously, and apply them to our daily lives:

"If my people, who are called by my name, will humble themselves and pray and seek my face and turn from their wicked ways, then will I hear from heaven and will forgive their sin and will heal their land." (2 Chronicles 7:14)

"If any of you lack wisdom, let him ask of God, that giveth to all men liberally, and upbraideth not; and it shall be given him." (James 1:5)

We also need to keep reminding ourselves that in due time, **every** knee will bow at the name of Jesus, and **every** tongue will confess that Jesus Christ is Lord. (Philippians 2:10-11)

Appendix B

Darwin's Deadly Legacy

The Bible speaks of God as being our Creator from Genesis to the book of Revelation. The theory of evolution denies the account of creation in the book of Genesis. As a result, it undermines people's trust in the Bible.

In addition, Jesus quoted from Genesis when answering a question about divorce. (See Matthew 19:1-12.) Since Jesus treated Genesis as being accurate and authoritative, to deny that God is our Creator, as described in the book of Genesis, undermines confidence in Jesus.

Darwin's theory of evolution is the origin of racism. The full title of the book, as originally published, is *On the Origin of Species by Means of Natural Selection, or the Preservation of **Favoured Races** in the Struggle for Life* (emphasis added).

Once people think in terms of some "races" being better than others, then it is natural to apply that to humans and wonder which ones are superior. Adolf Hitler was convinced that Jews, blacks, and Gypsies were inferior races that should be eliminated. The result of that was the Holocaust.[1]

Hitler also believed that the Aryans (blue-eyed blonds) were a superior race that should be increased. Therefore, he encouraged unmarried German girls to have sex with Aryan men in order to produce "superior" children. According to Kitty Werthman, who lived in Austria under Nazi occupation, "unwed mothers were glorified for having a baby for Hitler." [2]

An article titled "Darwin's Bodysnatchers" tells how people have been murdered in order to provide "specimens" for museums and for evolutionary research.[3] Following are some examples:

Darwin's Deadly Legacy

(1) British evolutionists believed that the Australian Aborigines were the "missing link." As a result, they paid people to kill them and ship their bodies to British museums. It is estimated that as many as 10,000 Aborigines were shipped to England.

(2) American evolutionists were also involved in the effort to get specimens of "subhumans." The Smithsonian Institution has the remains of 15,000 people of a variety of races.

(3) Museums not only displayed the bones of these people, they also stuffed their skins to use for displays. They had taxidermists treat these people as if they were animals.

(4) The curator of the Australian Museum in Sydney, Australia published a booklet which listed the Aborigines as being "Australian animals."

(5) Amelie Dietrich is a German evolutionist who has been called the "Angel of Black Death" because she had so many Aborigines shot in order to use them as specimens for her museum. She had taxidermists skin them, stuff them, and mount them for displays. This attitude reminds me too much of Hitler and his Nazi scientists.

(6) This kind of thing has become less common, but it has not entirely gone away. Even in quite modern times, some major institutions have been trying to get the bones of Aborigines.

Jesus told us that we would be able to recognize the nature of things by the kind of fruit that it bears. He said,

> "By their fruits ye shall know them." (Matthew 7:20)

Well, if you judge the theory of evolution by its fruits in the lives of men and nations, then it becomes obvious that this is a deadly deception.

Appendix C

Resources

How to Fight Discouragement by Maria Kneas (CreateSpace, 2015). This book has been helpful for people who are troubled by current events. It has also helped people with health problems, financial difficulties, relationship problems, etc.

Overcoming the War on Christians by Maria Kneas (CreateSpace, 2015).

The Criminalization of Christianity by Janet L. Folger (Multnomah Books, 2005).

Persecution by David Limbaugh (Harper Perennial, 2004).

The Marketing of Evil by David Kupelian (WND Books, 2005). The subtitle of this book speaks volumes about what is happening in our society. It is *How Radicals, Elitists, and Pseudo-Experts Sell Us Corruption Disguised As Freedom.*

Rise of the Warrior Cop by Radley Balko (PublicAffairs, 2013). The subtitle is *The Militarization of America's Police Forces.*

When A Nation Forgets God by Dr. Erwin Lutzer (Moody Publishers, 2009). This book shows a number of troubling parallels between modern America and Germany in the days before Hitler became a full-fledged dictator.

Tavistock Institute: Social Engineering the Masses by Daniel Estulin (Trine Day, 2015).

Standing Firm in the Faith by James L. Morrisson (my father) (CreateSpace, 2010).

Dad became a Christian when he was in his sixties, and he loved the Bible so much that he got a Master's degree in Biblical Studies. But there is a lot more to this book than that. Dad was fighting terminal cancer when he wrote the book. He has some insights that can only be gained in the trenches. You can read the entire book online:

www.StandingFirmInTheFaith.com.

Three of the chapters in this edition of *Prepare for Persecution* are based on material from *Standing Firm in the Faith*. They are a mixture of Dad's work and mine. (I contributed to Dad's book, and the copyright is in my name as well as his.) I made some changes to make the text easier to read, added some new material, and changed the Scripture quotes to the King James Version. Those three chapters are "Do We Love God?" and "Renewing Our Minds" and "A Biblical Approach to Pain."

If you search for *Standing Firm in the Faith* online, just use the title and my Dad's first name. His last name has an unusual spelling. Search engines "correct" it, and as a result, they then fail to find it because what they are looking for no longer matches his name.

Notice

My book *How to Prepare for Hard Times and Persecution* is another version of *Prepare for Persecution*. They are two variations of the same book, with some differences in content and presentation.

I recommend *Pepare for Persecution* for Doug Hagmann's listeners. Four chapters and one appendix were written with them in mind. Plus it has a *Foreword* by Doug Hagmann.

Notes

[NOTE: The easiest way to find these articles online is to search for the title. Sometimes typing the link doesn't work, especially if it has hyphens in it.]

Chapter 1. Understanding The Times

1. G. Brock Chisholm, "The Re-Establishment of Peacetime Society," *Psychiatry*, February 1946.

2. *Ibid.*

3. "The Courts Define Humanism as a Religion," by Arthur M. Jackson. This article was published in *The Humanist Institute Quarterly*, Winter 1987. www.arthurmjackson.com/rootsf.html

4. John Dunphy, *The Humanist*, January/February 1983. Cited in "Secular Humanists Give Dunphy Another Platform." www.eagleforum.org/educate/1995/nov95/dunphy.html

5. *Marriage and the Family*, The British Humanist Association, 1969. Cited by Dr. Dennis L. Cuddy, *The Globalists* (Oklahoma City: Hearthstone Publishing, 2001), p. 124.

6. "Humanist Manifesto I" (This is the original Humanist Manifesto, written in 1933. Other versions have been written since then.) http://americanhumanist.org/Humanism/Humanist_Manifesto_I

7. Ian T. Taylor, *In the Minds of Men*, 3rd edition (Toronto, Canada: TFE Publishing, 1991), p. 425.

8. "A New Way of Thinking," by Berit Kjos (chapter 3 from her book *Brave New Schools*). www.crossroad.to/Books/BraveNewSchools/3-NewThinking.htm

9. Thomas Sowell, "Indoctrinating the Children," in *Forbes*, February 1, 1993, p. 65.

10. *Ibid.*

11. G. Richard Bozarth, "On Keeping God Alive," *American Atheist*, November 1977.

12. "Yale Founded to Fight Liberalism."
www.christianity.com/church/church-history/timeline/1701-1800/yale-founded-to-fight-liberalism-11630185.html

13. "Yale Students Receive Bestiality, Incest Sensitivity Training During 'Sex Weekend,'" March 10, 2013
http://christiannews.net/2013/03/10/yale-students-receive-bestiality-incest-sensitivity-training-during-sex-weekend

"What the Yale? Ivy League Students Admit to Bestiality, Desires about Incest, During 'Sex Weekend' Workshop," March 6, 2013.
www.nydailynews.com/news/national/yale-students-admit-beatiality-sex-workshop-article-1.1280746

14. "Most Twentysomethings Put Christianity on the Shelf Following Spiritually Active Teen Years," September 11, 2006.
www.barna.org/barna-update/article/16-teensnext-gen/147-most-twentysomethings-put-christianity-on-the-shelf-following-spiritually-active-teen-years

"New Research Explores Teenage Views and Behavior Regarding the Supernatural," January 23, 2006.
www.barna.org/barna-update/article/5-barna-update/164-new-research-explores-teenage-views-and-behavior-regarding-the-supernatural

15. "Pedophilia the Next 'Sexual-Rights' Revolution? Academica, psychologists expanding LGBT argument to 'minor-attracted persons,'" January 2, 2014.
www.wnd.com/2014/01/pedophilia-the-next-sexual-rights-revolution

16. "Nurse Sues Hospital Over Forced Abortion Assist," April 20, 2010.
www.nydailynews.com/new-york/nurse-sues-hospital-forced-abortion-assist-article-1.448478

"Can the ACLU Force Catholic Hospitals to Perform Abortions?" December 5, 2013.
www.washingtontimes.com/news/2013/dec/5/knight-treating-the-mother-by-killing-the-baby

"President Obama Starts Process of Removing Doctors' Protections on Abortions," January 1, 2009.
www.lifenews.com/2009/01/01/nat-4865

17. "Supreme Court Sets Date for Hobby Lobby's Challenge to Obama's HHS Mandate," January 8, 2014.
www.lifenews.com/2014/01/08/supreme-court-sets-date-for-hobby-lobbys-challenge-to-obamas-hhs-mandate

18. "State 'Imposing' Its 'Gay' Beliefs on Cake Artist," January 7, 2014.
www.wnd.com/2014/01/state-imposing-its-gay-beliefs-on-cake-artist

"Judge to Colorado Baker: Bake Cakes For Gay 'Weddings'… Or Else," December 10, 2013.
www.lifesitenews.com/news/judge-to-colorado-baker-bake-a-cake-for-gay-weddings...or-else

"'Tolerance' Now Means Government-Coerced Celebration," December 16, 2013.
www.wnd.com/2013/12/tolerance-now-means-govt-coerced-celebration

"Baker Says He's Rather Go to Jail After Judge Orders Him to Bake Cakes for Gay 'Weddings.'" December 11, 2013.
www.lifesitenews.com/news/baker-says-hed-rather-go-to-jail-after-judge-orders-him-to-bake-cakes-for-g

"Judge: 'Gay Rights' Trump 1st Amendment," December 10, 2013.
www.wnd.com/2013/12/judge-gay-rights-trump-1st-amendment-for-christians/

19. "NM Court Says Christian Photographers Must Compromise Beliefs," August 22, 2013.
http://radio.foxnews.com/toddstarnes/top-stories/nm-court-says-christian-photographers-must-compromise-beliefs.html

"NM Supreme Court: Price of Citizenship Is Compromising Your Feliefs," August 22, 2013.
http://www.adfmedia.org/News/PRDetail/8469

20. Government Shutdown Results in Ban on Military Chaplains," October 11, 2013.
www.militarydefensefirm.com/Military-Criminal-Defense-Blog/2013/October/Government-Shutdown-Results-in-Ban-on-Military-C.aspx

21. "Pentagon May Court Martial Soldiers Who Share Christian Faith," May 1, 2013.
www.breitbart.com/Big-Peace/2013/05/01/Breaking-Pentagon-Confirms-Will-Court-Martial-Soldiers-Who-Share-Christian-Faith

22. "Chaplain Punished for Sharing His Faith in Suicide Prevention Class," December 9, 2014.
www.foxnews.com/opinion/2014/12/09/chaplain-punished-for-sharing-his-faith-in-suicide-prevention-class.html

23. "Marine Court Martialed for Refusing to Remove Bible Verse," May 26, 2015.
www.foxnews.com/opinion/2015/05/26/marine-court-martialed-for-refusing-to-remove-bible-verse.html

24. *A Clear and Present Danger: The Threat to Religious Liberty in the Military*, the Family Research Council, March 21, 2014. (This is a 21-page document that takes a long time to download. You may have to try doing it several times.)
http://downloads.frc.org/EF/EF14C52.pdf

25. "Shooter's Anti-Christian Motive Missed & Noted."
www.mediaresearch.org/cyberalerts/1999/cyb19990917.asp

26. "Fort Worth Shootings: Tragedy at an Unarmed Church"
http://reformed-theology.org/html/issue10/hate_crime.htm

27. "Shooter's Anti-Christian Motive Missed & Noted."
www.mediaresearch.org/cyberalerts/1999/cyb19990917.asp

"Do You Believe in God?" April 26, 1999. (Christian teenagers were shot at Columbine High School in Littleton, Colorado after being asked if they believed in God, and answering "Yes.")
www.worldnetdaily.com/news/article.asp?ARTICLE_ID=14726

Chapter 2. Brainwashing Christians

1. "Baker Who Refused Same-Sex Couple Must Take Sensitivity Training," by Dave Bohon, June 6, 2014.
www.thenewamerican.com/culture/faith-and-morals/item/18431-baker-who-refused-same-sex-couple-must-take-sensitivity-training

2. *Ibid.*

3. *Ibid.*

4. *Ibid.*

5. "When the State Owns Your Soul," by Lee Duigon, June 19, 2014.
www.newswithviews.com/Duigon/lee256.htm

6. "Government to Farmers: Host Same-Sex Wedding or Pay a $13,000 Fine," August 19. 2014.
http://dailysignal.com/2014/08/19/government-farmers-host-sex-wedding-pay-13000-fine

[NOTE: The most serious problem is not the fine. It is forcing them to take "re-education" classes in order to change their religious and moral convictions. In other words, it is brainwashing and persecution.]

Chapter 3. Thought Police In Colleges

1. L. Ron Hubbard, "Propaganda by Redefinition of Words," October 5, 1971. Cited in "Hubbard in His Own Words."
www.xenu.net/archive/infopack/5.htm

2. "University to Students: 'All Whites Are Racist.': Mandatory Program 'Treats' Politically Incorrect Attitudes," October 30, 2007.
www.worldnetdaily.com/news/article.asp?ARTICLE_ID=58426

3. *Ibid.*

4. Video: "Think What We Think… Or Else: Thought Control on the American Campus"
www.youtube.com/watch?v=6EbQfmVoOfM

5. "William Wilberforce (1759-1833)"
www.brycchancarey.com/abolition/wilberforce.htm

6. "James Reeb"
http://en.wikipedia.org/wiki/James_J._Reeb

7. "University Drops 'Whites Are Racist' Plan: Prez Says: 'I have directed that the program be stopped immediately,'" November 1, 2007.
www.wnd.com/index.php?fa=PAGE.view&pageId=44340

8. "'All Whites Racist' Indoctrination Revived!" May 28, 2008.
www.wnd.com/index.php?fa=PAGE.printable&pageId=65532

9. "Teaching Plan: America 'an Oppressive Hellhole': University Outlines 'Re-education' for Those Who Hold 'Wrong'Views," November 27, 2009.
www.wnd.com/index.php?fa=PAGE.printable&pageId=117313

Letter to University of Minnesota
www.crossroad.to/Quotes/Education/re-learning/
letter-u-minnesota.htm

10 "At U, Future Teachers May Be Reeducated: They Must Denounce Exclusionary Biases and Embrace the Vision (Or else)," November 22, 2009.
www.startribune.com/opinion/commentary/70662162.html

Chapter 4. Teaching Kids To Be Sociopaths

1. "'Beach week' Draws Black Crowd—and Violence," April 30, 2013
www.wnd.com/2013/04/beach-week-draws-black-crowd-and-violence

2. "'Abortion Battles' Game Caught on Video"
www.youtube.com/watch?v=78rYupgxxoI

3. "Teens Caught on Tape Laughing About Sexually Abusing and Urinating on Underage Girl"
www.youtube.com/watch?v=d9-JARpqoj4

Chapter 5. A Biblical Warning For America

1. "Wicca Infiltrates the Churches—Wiccan Rituals Gaining Popularity in Christian Churches" by Catherine Edwards, *Insight on the News*, Dec 6, 1999.
http://findarticles.com/p/articles/mi_m1571/is_45_15/ai_58050620

Notes

2. "Middle School Girls Forced to Ask Classmates for 'Lesbian Kiss' During Anti-Bullying Presentation," April 20, 2013.
http://christiannews.net/2013/04/20/middle-school-girls-forced-to-ask-classmates-for-lesbian-kiss-during-anti-bullying-presentation

3. "Two Kindergarten Five-Year-Olds Caught Having Sex in Bathroom," February 25, 2014.
www.examiner.com/article/two-kindergarten-5-year-olds-caught-having sex-bathroom-teacher-may-be-fired

4. "Sex and the Public Schools," February 24, 2014.
http://endoftheamericandream.com/archives/sex-and-the-public-schools

5. "Abortion's Toll of 55 Million Called 'Genocide,'" January 21, 2014.
www.wnd.com/2014/01/abortions-toll-of-55-million-called-genocide

6. Dr. Ginette Paris discusses her book *The Sacrament of Abortion* on her website. She is a psychologist, a therapist, and a professor at the Pacifica Institute in Santa Barbara, California. She is also a pagan. Her website includes sections on "pagan meditations" and "pagan grace."
www.ginetteparis.com/psychologyofabortion/
readexcerptonabortion.html

7. "Pedophilia the Next 'Sexual-Rights' Rebolution? Academia, Psychologists Expanding LGBT Argument to 'Minor-Attracted Persons,'" January 2, 2014.
www.wnd.com/2014/01/pedophilia-the-next-sexual-rights-revolution

8. "New Research Explores Teenage Views and Behavior Regarding the Supernatural," January 23, 2006.
www.barna.org/barna-update/article/5-barna-update/164-new-research-explores-teenage-views-and-behavior-regarding-the-supernatural

9. "Sex and the Public Schools," February 24, 2014.
http://endoftheamericandream.com/archives/sex-and-the-public-schools

10. "Unveiling the Global Interfaith Agenda," October 2, 2011.
www.crossroad.to/articles2/forcing-change/11/interfaith.htm

11. I found all of these attempts to mix Christianity with other religions by doing a quick search on the Internet. You can easily find them for yourself. Just search for "Christian" plus any other religion or spiritual practice that you can think of.

12. "Barna Survey Examines Changes in Worldview Among Christians over the Past 13 Years," March 6, 2009.
www.barna.org/barna-update-21-transformation-252-barna-survey-examines-changes-in-worldview-among-christians-over-the-past-13-years

Chapter 6. Heading Towards Dictatorship

1. "Socialism vs. Freedom." (Video of a talk by Kitty Werthmann)
www.sdfamily.org/Kitty+Wetrthmann

2. "Adolf Hitler and Charismatic Leadership."
http://eeuropeanhistory.suite101.com/article.cfm/adolf_hitler_and_charmismatic_leadership

3. Hitler with a little girl.
www.fpp.co.uk/Hitler/images/children/Inge_Terboven_on_Hitler.jpg

Hitler with a baby.
www.golivewire.com/forums/img.cgi?i=62823

4. "Don't Let Freedom Slip Away: Sobering Steps from Freedom to Fascism." (Kitty Werthmann)
www.crossroad.to/articles2/010/fascism.htm

5. "National ID: Another Step to Totalitarianism."
www.wnd.com/index.php?fa=PAGE.printable&pageId=45536

6. "Biometric National ID Card Could Be Mandated on All American Workers," March 28, 2013.
www.naturalnews.com/039683_biometric_national_id_card_mandatory.html

7. "Cradle-to-Career Plan by Obama and Duncan."
www.crossroad.to/articles2/010/edwatch/garner/1-cradle-to-grave.htm

8. "Court Orders Christian Child into Government Education: 10-Year-Old's 'Vigorous' Defense of Her Faith Condemned by Judge."
www.wnd.com/index.php?fa=PAGE.printable&pageId=108084

9. "Where's the Outrage Over What Just Happened to Student Loans?"
www.foxnews.com/opinion/2010/03/26/dana-perino-student-loans-health-care-sen-kent-conrad-democrats-students/

10. "Eye-Popping Power Grab: Licensing of U.S. Colleges: Federal Scheme Poses 'Greatest Threat to Academic Freedom in our Lifetime.'"
www.wnd.com/index.php?fa=PAGE.view&pageId=209589

11. "Chrysler Files to Seek Bankruptcy Protection."
www.nytimes.com/2009/05/01/business/01auto.html

12. "Plan to Ax Dealers Not Chrysler's Decision."
www.reuters.com/article/idUSN2632731920090526

13. "Eugenics and the Nazis—the California Connection."
www.waragainsttheweak.com/offSiteArchive/www.sfgate.com

14. "5 People Die under New Washington Physician-Assisted Suicide Law."
www.ama-assn.org/amednews/2009/07/06/prsc0706.htm"

15. "Have Researched Euthanasia Speak Out."
www.hospicepatients.org/euth-experts-speak.html

16. "'The Weekend Cleanup: The Gruesome Aftermath of Legalized Euthanasia in Belgium."
www.lifesitenews.com/ldn/2009/jun/09060109.html

17. "Obama's Health Rationer-in-Chief: White House Health-Care Adviser Ezekiel Emanuel Blames the Hippocratic Oath for the 'Overuse' of Medical Care."
http://online.wsj.com/article/SB10001424052970203706604574374463280098676.html

18. "Palin Firestorm Brings Fresh Scrutiny to ObamaCare 'Death Panels.'"
www.lifesitenews.com/ldn/2009/aug/09081109.html

19. "Eric Holder: Gun Grabber."
http://97.74.65.51/readArticle.aspx?ARTID=33694

20. "Obama, the U.N., and the Right to Bear Arms."
http://canadafreepress.com/index.php/article/18882

21. "Obama Declares War on Free Speech"
www.humanevents.com/article.php?print=yes&id=33869

22. "FCC Commissioner: Return of Fairness Doctrine Could Control Web Content."
www.businessandmedia.org/printer/2008/20080812160747.aspx

23. "Inspired by Saul Alinsky, FCC 'Diversity' Chief Calls for 'Confrontational Movement' to Give Public Broadcasting Dominant Role in Communications."
http://cnsnews.com/news/article/53055

24. "FCC 'Diversity' Czar on Chavez's Venezuela: 'Incredible Democratic Revolution.'" (This article includes a video of Mark Lloyd's statement.)
http://newsbusters.org/blogs/seton-motley/2009/08/28/video-fcc-diversity-czar-chavezs-venezuela-incredible-democratic-revol

25. "Wave Goodbye to Internet Freedom: FCC Crosses the Rubicon into Online Regulation."
www.washingtontimes.com/news/2010/dec/2/wave-goodbye-to-internet-freedom

26. "FCC Commissioner Copps Proposes 'Public Value Test.'"
www.heartland.org/infotech-news.org/article/28940/FCC_Commissioner_Copps_Proposes_Public_Value_Test.html

27. "US Planning to Recruit One in 24 Americans as Citizen Spies."
www.smh.com.au/articles/2002/07/14/1026185141232.html

28. "Your Friendly Community Spies."
www.crossroad.to/articles2/2002/spy.html

29. "The War on Hate Bans Christian Values."
www.crossroad.to/text/articles/cwhbcv3-98.html

30. "Smartphone."
http://en.wikipedia.org/wiki/Smartphone

31. "How to Take Better Pictures with Your Smartphone's Camera."
http://lifehacker.com/5662812/how-to-take-better-pictures-with-your-smartphones-camera

32. "iPhone."
http://en.wikipedia.org/wiki/IPhone

33. "I Spy: Controversial PatriotApp Lets Citizens Alert the Feds."
www.livescience.com/technology/patriot-app-iphone-101214.html

34. "Mobilizing the Globe" [PatriotApp].
http://patriotapps.com/PatriotApp.html

35. "Bush Makes Power Grab."
www.wnd.com/index.php?fa=PAGE.printable&pageId=41728

36. "Hidden Threats—Part I."
www.wnd.com/index.php?fa=PAGE.printable&pageId=6111

37. "Detention Camps on American Soil."
www.rutherford.org/articles_db/commentary.asp?record_id=400

38. "North American Army Created without OK by Congress: U.S., Canada Ink Deal to Fight Domestic Emergencies."
www.wnd.com/index.php?fa=PAGE.printable&pageId=57228

39. "A UN Militia in Your Community?"
www.crossroad.to/text/articles/rapid-reaction99.htm

40. "Bill Creates Detention Camps in U.S. for 'Emergencies': Sweeping, Undefined Purpose Raises Worries about Military Police State."
www.wnd.com/index.php?fa=PAGE.printable&pageId=87757

41. "Is the US Government Preparing to Send Dissenters to Prison Camps?"
www.newswithviews.com/NWV-News/news123.htm

42. "Big Brother Loves 'Financial Reform.'"
www.washingtontimes.com/news/2010/apr/30/big-brother-loves-financial-reform/print/

43. "Financial Regulatory Windfall."
http://spectator.org/archives/2010/04/30/financial-regulatory-windfall/print

44. "New 'Safety Plan' Would Control What You Eat."
www.wnd.com/index.php?fa=PAGE.printable&pageId=146957

45. "Federal Agents Invade Farm for 5 a.m. Milk Inspection."
www.wnd.com/index.php?fa=PAGE.printable&pageId=144557

46. "Future of the News."
www.americanthinker.com/2010/07/future_of_the_news.html

47. "Obama's 'Big Brother' Vanishes from Speech: 'Civilian Security Force' Missing from 'Call to Service' Transcript."
www.wnd.com/index.php?fa=PAGE.view&pageId =69784

[NOTE: This article has an embedded video of the speech. Obama's call for a Civilian Security Force was omitted from the transcript of the speech, as published by the media.]

48. "Civilian Security Force on Agenda Again."
www.wnd.com/index.php?fa=PAGE.view&pageId=92109

49. "Obamacare Prescription: 'Emergency Health Army.'"
www.wnd.com/index.php?fa=PAGE.view&pageId=132001

50. "Obama Just Got His Private Army."
http://frontpage.americandaughter.com/?p=3549

51."Democrat: Let's Have Mandatory National Service."
www.wnd.com/index.php?fa=PAGE.view&pageId=184325

52. Rep. Rangel proposed this same bill in 2006 and 2007. Its provisions are discussed in "The Draft is Back—Again! 'Universal National Service Act of 2006.'"
www.crossroad.to/articles2/006/draft.htm

53. National Security Letter,
http://en.wikipedia.org/wiki/National_Security_Letter

54. Judge Andrew Napolitano, Natural Rights Patriot Act—Part 3 of 3
www.youtube.com/watch_popup?v=7n2m-X7OIuY

[NOTE: The information begins at 2:01 minutes, starting with the sentence, "Do you know that the Congress has used the Commerce Clause to make it a crime for you to speak the truth?"]

55. Charles Krauthammer, "Government by Regulation," December 31, 2010.
www.nationalreview.com/articles/256104/government-regulation-charles-krauthammer

56. "White House Presses for New Climate, Wilderness Protections," The Washington Post, December 24, 2010.
www.washingtonpost.com/wp-dyn/content/article/
2010/12/23/AR2010122305643.html

57. "Media Excuse Obama's Power Grab," December 26, 2010.
www.aim.org/aim-column/media-excuse-obama%e2%80%99s-power-grab/

[NOTE: Because of the strange codes used for the apostrophe in the Internet address, the easiest way to find this article is to search for the title plus "aim.org"]

58. Center for American Progress, "The Power of the President: Recommendations to Advance Progressive Change," November 16, 2010.
www.americanprogress.org/issues/2010/11/executive_orders.html

59. "Medicare Regulation Revives End-of-Life Planning," December 25, 2010.
http://washingtonexaminer.com/politics/2010/12/medicare-regulation-revives-end-life-planning

60. Charles Krauthammer, "Government by Regulation," December 31, 2010.
www.nationalreview.com/articles/256104/
government-regulation-charles-krauthammer

61. "SWAT Team conducts food raid in rural Ohio."
www.crossroad.to/articles2/08/swat-team.htm

Chapter 7. Mainstreaming Occultism

1. Catherine Edwards, "Wicca Infiltrates the Churches," December 6, 1999. (Originally from Insight Magazine, Vol. 15, No. 45.)
http://www.confessingumc.org/news-events/wicca-infiltrates-the-churches/

2. "Satanist Church Rents Out Oklahoma City Civic Center for Exorcism," September 1, 2010. (This article is two pages. The link below goes to the first one, which leads to the second.)
http://abcnews.go.com/US/satanist-church-rents-oklahoma-civic-center-exorcis-ritual/story?id=11524098

3. "Plans for 'Black Mass' at Harvard Anger Boston Catholics," May 9, 2014.
www.reuters.com/article/2014/05/09/us-usa-harvard-satanists-idUSBREA480OD20140509

"Amid Outcry, Black Mass at Harvard Is Called Off," May 13, 2014.
www.bostonglobe.com/metro/2014/05/12/cardinal-sean-malley-expresses-disappointment-harvard-decision-allow-black-mass-campus/tUjYx2817C65LAHousRIeP/story.html

4. "Devil-Worship Group Unveils Satanic Statue Design for Oklahoma State Capitol," January 7, 2014.
www.nydailynews.com/news/politics/devil-worship-group-unveils-satanic-statue-design-oklahoma-state-capitol-article-1.1568893

5. "Deceived by a Counterfeit 'Jesus': The Twisted 'Truths' of *The Shack* and *A Course in Miracles*."
www.crossroad.to/articles2/08/shack.htm

6. "The Clergy Project."
www.clergyproject.org/

7. "Dark Horse (Katy Perry Song)."
http://en.wikipedia.org/wiki/Dark_Horse_(Katy_Perry_song)

"Katy Perry & Juicy J Are Fiery Satanists As They Perform 'Dark Horse' At The 2014 Grammys!" January 26, 2014.
http:perezhilton.com/2014-01-26-grammys-2014-katy-perry-performs-dark-horse-juicy-j

8. "Fox Network Launching New TV Series That Glorifies Lucifer; Marketed with Pro-Satan Tweets," May 24, 2015.
www.naturalnews.com/049831_Lucifer_Fox_mainstream_media.html

9. "Lucifer (TV Series)," Wikipedia.
https://en.wikipedia.org/wiki/Lucifer_(TV_series)

10. "Satanic Prayer Disrupted at City Council Meeting," WEAR-TV, July 15, 2016. This article includes a video.
http://weartv.com/news/local/satanic-prayer-at-council-meeting-disrupted-by-crowd

11. "Satanic Group Set to Lead Phoenix City Council in Prayer," Fox News, January 29, 2016.
http://www.foxnews.com/us/2016/01/29/satanic-group-set-to-lead-phoenix-city-council-in-prayer.html

Chapter 8. Bathroom Battles and College Chaos

1. Catherine E. Lhamon (Assistant Secretary for Civil Rights, U.S. Department of Education) and Vanita Gupta (Principal Deputy Assistant Attorney General for Civil Rights, U.S. Department of Justice), "Dear Colleague Letter on Transgender Students," May 13, 2016.
www2.ed.gov/about/offices/list/ocr/letters/colleague-201605-title-ix-transgender.pdf

2. U.S. Department of Justice, Office of Public Affairs, "U.S. Departments of Justice and Education Release Joint Guidance to Help Schools Ensure the Civil Rights of Transgender Students," May 13, 2016.
www.justice.gov/opa/pr/us-departments-justice-and-education-release-joint-guidance-help-schools-ensure-civil-rights

3. Lauren Booker, "What It Means to be Gender-Fluid," CNN, April 13, 2016.
www.cnn.com/2016/04/13/living/gender-fluid-feat/index.html

4. Peter Hasson, "New York City Lets You Choose from 31 Different Gender Identities," Daily Caller, May 24, 2016.
http://dailycaller.com/2016/05/24/new-york-city-lets-you-choose-from-31-different-gender-identities

5. Amanda Casanova, "11 States Sue over Obama's Transgender Directive," *Religion Today*, May 26, 2016.
www.christianheadlines.com/blog/11-states-sue-over-obama-s-transgender-directive.html

6. Ben Johnson, "The Most Dangerous, and Underreported, Part of Obama's Transgender Edict," LifeSiteNews, May 20, 2016.
www.lifesitenews.com/blogs/not-just-bathrooms-the-most-dangerous-and-underreported-part-of-obamas-tran

7. Gary J. Gates, "How Many People Are Lesbian, Gay, Bisexual, and Transgender?" Williams Institute, April 2011.
http://williamsinstitute.law.ucla.edu/research/census-lgbt-demographics-studies/how-many-people-are-lesbian-gay-bisexual-and-transgender

8. Peter LaBarbera, "'Gay' Power vs. Religious Liberty," WorldNetDaily, November 29, 2013.
www.wnd.com/2013/11/gay-power-vs-religious-liberty

9. David Kupelian, "What's Really behind America's Transgender Mania?" WorldNetDaily, May 15, 2016.
www.wnd.com/2016/05/whats-really-behind-americas-transgender-mania

10. David Kupelian, *The Snapping of the American Mind* (Washington DC: WND Books, 2015), p. 171.

11. Claire Chretien, "Bathrooms Are Just the Beginning: A Scary Look into the Trans Movement's End Goals," LifeSiteNews, May 6, 2016.
www.lifesitenews.com/news/bathrooms-are-just-the-beginning-a-scary-look-into-the-trans-movements-end

12. Riki Wilchins, "We'll Win the Bathroom Battle When the binary Burns," *The Advocate*, April 29, 2016.
www.advocate.com/commentary/2016/4/29/well-win-bathroom-battle-when-binary-burns

13. Traci G. Lee and Melissa Harris Perry, "Being Tansgender No Longer a 'Mental Disorder': APA," NBC News, December 7, 2012.
www.nbcnews.com/id/50075205/t/being-transgender-no-longer-mental-disorder-apa

14. Jack Minor, "'Gay' Laws Set Stage for Pedophilia 'Rights,'" WorldNetDaily, July 18, 2013.
www.wnd.com/2013/07/gay-laws-set-stage-for-pedophilia-rights

15. Thomas Francis, "Those Who Practice Bestiality Say They're Part of the Next Sexual Rights Movement," August 20, 2009.
www.browardpalmbeach.com/news/those-who-practice-bestiality-say-theyre-part-of-the-next-sexual-rights-movement-6334747

16. Berit Kjos, "A New Way of thinking."
www.crossroad.to/Books/BraveNewSchools/3-NewThinking.htm

17. Thomas Sowell, "Indoctrinating the Children," in *Forbes*, February 1, 1993, p. 65.

18. Ibid.

19. Michael Bastasch, "California Lawmaker Poised to Make it Illegal to Question Global Warming," Daily Caller, June 2, 2016.
www.dailycaller.com/2016/06/02/california-lawmakers-poised-to-make-it-illegal-to-question-global-warming

20. Eric Owens, "US College Professor Demands Imprisonment for Climate-Change Deniers," Daily Caller, March 17, 2014.
http://dailycaller.com/2014/03/17/u-s-college-professor-demands-imprisonment-for-climate-change-deniers

21. S. Noble, "Senator Whitehouse Wants global Warming Deniers in Prison," Independent Sentinel, June 26, 2015.
www.independentsentinel.com/senator-whitehouse-wants-global-warming-deniers-in-prison

22. Bob Unruh, "See Obama Admit Seeking Advice from Communist," WorldNetDaily, April 15, 2015.
www.wnd.com/2015/04/see-obama-admit-seeking-counsel-from-communist

23. Judi McLeod, "Saul Alinsky's Son: 'Obama Learned His Lesson Well,'" Canada Free Press, September 2, 2008.
www.canadafreepress.com/article/saul-alinskys-son-obama-learned-his-lesson-well

24. Berit Kjos, "Quotes and Excerpts from *Rules for Radicals* by Saul Alinsky–1971."
www.crossroad.to/Quotes/communism/alinsky.htm

25. Donna Calvin, "the 45 Communist Goals as Read into the Congressional Record, 1963," April 2011.
www.beliefnet.com/columnists/watchwomanonthewall/2011/04/the-45-communist-goals-as-read-into-the-congressional-record-1963.html

26. The British Humanist Association, *Marriage and the Family*, 1969. Cited by Dr. Dennis L. Cuddy, *The Globalists* (Oklahoma City, OK: Hearthstone Publishing, 2001), p. 124.

Chapter 9. Dealing With Shock

1. "Baker Faces Prison for Refusing to Bake Same-Sex Wedding Cake," December 12, 2013.
www.breitbart.com/Big-Government/2013/12/12/Christian-Baker-Willing-To-Go-to-Jail-for-Declining-Gay-Wedding-Cake

Chapter 10. Fighting Fear

1. "Military Warned 'Evangelicals' No. 1 Threat: Christians Targeted Ahead of Muslim Brotherhood, Al-Quaida, KKK," April 5, 2013.
www.wnd.com/2014/04/military-warned-evangelicals-no-1-threat

"Colorado State Police and Homeland Security Target Christians As Anti-Patriots," April 9, 2013.
www.saveamericafoundation.com/2013/04/04/breaking-news-colorado-state-police-and-homeland-security-target-christians-as-anti-patriots

"Army Reserve Presentation Calls Christians 'Extremists,'" April 5, 2013.
www.worldmag.com/2013/04/army_reserve_presentation_calls_christians_extremists

"Pro-Lifers Should Be Concerned About Obama Assassination List: Judge Napolitano," February 6, 2013.
www.lifesitenews.com/news/will-pro-life-errorists-be-names-to-obamas-assassination-list

"72 Types Of Americans That Are Considered 'Potential Terrorists' In Official Government Documents,," August 26, 2013.
http://thetruthwins.com/archives/72-types-of-americans-that-are-considered-potential-terrorists-in-official-government-documents

[NOTE: This last article has links to many of the documents. Now that this information has been made public, I would not be surprised if the online versions of these documents have been modified, with the relevant text either deleted or changed. That would be an effective way to create "plausible deniability." In addition, some of these documents may have been removed from the Internet.]

Chapter 12. The Bottom Line

1. The Clergy Project is an online support group for pastors who are atheists. Their motto is "Moving beyond faith."
www.clergyproject.org

Chapter 14. Building Faith

1. Sir William Ramsay, *The Bearing Of Recent Discovery On The Trustworthiness Of The New Testament*, (Hodder & Stoughton, 1915), p. 85.

2. *Op cit.*, p. 89.

3. *Op cit.*, p. 222.

4. *Ibid.*

Chapter 17. Don't Give The Devil A Beachhead

1. In 1981, John Keating published a book titled *Strength Under Control: Meekness and Zeal*.

Chapter 18. Giving Thanks To God

1. G. Richard Bozarth, "On Keeping God Alive," *American Atheist*, November 1977. He said: "We must ask how we can kill the God of Christianity."

2. "Baker Faces Prison for Refusing to Bake Same-Sex Wedding Cake," December 12, 2013.
www.breitbart.com/Big-Government/2013/12/12/Christian-Baker-Willing-To-Go-to-Jail-for-Declining-Gay-Wedding-Cake

Chapter 22. The Antidote To Humanism

1. Dr. Peter S. Cook, "Summary-Review of *The Fateful Hoaxing of Margaret Mead: A Historical Analysis of Her Samoan Research* by Derek Freeman," October 31, 2010.
https://antioligarch.wordpress.com/2010/10/31/the-fateful-hoaxing-of-margaret-mead-a-historical-analysis-of-her-samoan-research/

NOTE: Dr. Cook's exposure of this fraud is very valuable, but he seems to be a materialist who doesn't comprehend that God has given us a conscience. His analysis ignores (and perhaps denies) the spiritual aspect of life.

2. Carl Wieland, "Darwin's Bodysnatchers," *Creation Ex Nihilo*, Vol. 14, No. 2, March-May 1992. This article is also available online. http://creation.com/darwins-bodysnatchers-new-horrors

3. Dr. Jerry Bergman, "Darwinism and the Nazi Race Holocaust," November 1, 1999. https://answersingenesis.org/charles-darwin/racism/darwinism-and-the-nazi-race-holocaust/

4. Ellis Washington, "Sigmund Freud's Legacy of Perversity," October 21, 2011. (When I was in college, I took some classes in psychology. What this article says about Freud confirms what I studied about him.) http://www.wnd.com/2011/10/358637/

5. "Carl Jung, Alchemy, Taoism and Neo-Gnosticism." Jung received his information from at least three spirit guides. This article has quotes and excerpts from Jung's writings, with links to the sources. http://www.crossroad.to/Quotes/spirituality/jung.htm

Appendix A. Goddess Worship In America

1. Philip G. Davis, *Goddess Unmasked: The Rise of Neopagan Feminist Spirituality* (Dallas, Texas: Spence Publishing Company, 1999), chapters 2 through 12.

2. *Ibid.*, chapters 2, 11 and 12.

3. *Ibid.*, p. ix.

4. *Ibid.*, p. 360.
5. *Ibid.*

6. Information obtained by phone from the Public Information Office of the Statue of Liberty.

7. This poster is in the Valentine Museum in Richmond, Virginia. A picture of it appeared in the *Richmond Times-Dispatch*, September 29, 1998, p. D-1.

Notes

8. The National Academy of Sciences (articles with photos)

The Main Foyer and the Great Hall. This says that the architecht wanted to create a "temple of science."
www.nasonline.org/about-nas/visiting/nas/nas-building/the-main-foyer-and-the-great.html

The Great Hall. This shows pictures of some of the goddesses. You can see that the ceiling looks like a cathedral rather than a science building.
www.nasonline.org/about-nas/visiting-nas/nas-building/the-great-hall.html

9. *Op. cit.* Davis, p. 334.

10. *Ibid.*

11. *Ibid.*, pp. 336-337.

12. *Ibid.*, p. 341.

13. *Ibid.*, p. 343.

14. William Schnoebelen, *Wicca* (Ontario, California: Chick Publications, 1990).

15. *Op. cit.* Davis, pp. 3-4, 28-29.

16. *Ibid.*, p. 29.

17. *Ibid.*, pp. 24-25, 27.

18. *Ibid.*, pp. 24-25.

19. *Ibid.*, pp. 25-27.

20. *Ibid.*, pp. 29-31.

21. *Ibid.*, p. 31.

22. *Ibid.*, pp. 361, 363.

23. *Ibid.*, p. 361.

24. *Ibid.*, pp. 31-33.

25. Charlene E. Wheeler and Peggy L. Chinn, *Peace and Power: A Handbook of Feminist Process*, 3rd ed. (New York: National League for Nursing), pp. xi-xii. Quoted in *Goddess Unmasked*, p. 32.

26. "Halloween: Its Origins and Customs."
www.jeremiahproject.com/halloween.txt

Appendix B. Darwin's Deadly Legacy

1. Dr. Jerry Bergman, "Darwinism and the Nazi Race Holocaust," November 1, 1999.
https://answersingenesis.org/charles-darwin/racism/darwinism-and-the-nazi-race-holocaust/

2. Kitty Werthman, "Don't Let Freedom Slip Away," January 26, 2010. (The quotation is from the third paragraph that comes under the side heading "Hitler Targets Education – Eliminates Religious Instruction for Children.")
http://www.crossroad.to/articles2/010/fascism.htm

3. Carl Wieland, "Darwin's Bodysnatchers," *Creation Ex Nihilo*, Vol. 14, No. 2, March-May 1992. This article is also available online.
http://creation.com/darwins-bodysnatchers-new-horrors

*"If God be for us,
who can be against us?"*
(Romans 8:31)

Made in the USA
Columbia, SC
26 April 2017